Praise

'This book is the definitive resou
looking to break free from the grip of imposter
syndrome and achieve their most ambitious goals.
Finally, a book that truly delivers on its promise
to outsmart imposter syndrome and unlock your
full potential.'
— **Marianne Page**, CEO, author of *Simple,
Logical, Repeatable* and *Mission to Manage*

'*Outsmart Imposter Syndrome* goes a long way to
helping you dismantle an illusory myth. I like how
it is guides you meticulously step-by-step through
and out of the labyrinth. I believe the value in this
book is the careful explanations, the education and
the reassuring way it raises your self-awareness to
alert that an imposter syndrome assault has been
activated; how it is impacting your responses to
situations and life… and why and how to extract
yourself from its clutches.

This is a must-have self-care reference that will
augment any expert treatment.'
— **Andrew Priestley**, Leadership Coach, Grad
Dip Psych

'This book is an excellent guide for anyone who is
dealing with imposter syndrome. Written in a warm,
conversational style, with plenty of case studies and
references to academic work that back up what she
is saying.

Tara sets out a clear, step-by-step framework for identifying, calming and overcoming imposter syndrome. It is also a good book for understanding interpersonal psychology and relationships. Everyone can benefit from that, which makes this a must-read book.'
— **David B Horne**, Entrepreneur, author of *Add Then Multiply* and *Funded Female Founders*

'Tara's passion and dedication to understanding the root cause of imposter syndrome shines through in her book. While many experts advise pushing through discomfort, Tara's extensive experience and research offers a confident, efficient and strategic cure. This enjoyable read is highly recommended for everyone, as we all know someone who could benefit from the exceptional knowledge shared within.'
— **Fanny Snaith**, Money Life Coach

'This book is amazing. A perfect blend of theory and practical application means that you don't just read it, you action it, make huge discoveries about what's holding you back, and have the tools to free you up from the weight of feeling not good enough.
— **Julie Hutchison**, Team Performance Coach, Think Be Do Leadership

'Absolutely outstanding. Both pragmatic and deeply insightful.'
— **Mike Killen**, Owner, Sell Your Service, and author of *Five Figure Funnels*

OUTSMART IMPOSTER SYNDROME

End the suffering
Free your mind
Claim your inner success

TARA HALLIDAY

R^{e}think

First published in Great Britain in 2023
by Rethink Press (www.rethinkpress.com)

Cover image © Shutterstock | Jezper

Contents

Introduction   1
  Discoveries   3
  The roadmap   7

1 The Reality Of Imposter Syndrome   13
  What is imposter syndrome?   17
  Imposter syndrome symptoms   22
  Real solutions   25

2 Still The Storm   27
  Activated nervous system   28
  Neuroregulation   38

3 Calm Imposter Triggers   45
  Imposter activity   46

Circumstances   49

Challenges and the nervous system   54

4 **Relax Imposter Behaviours**   **65**

Hiding behaviours   68

Striving behaviours   76

Gradual exposure   82

5 **Freedom Framework**   **93**

Beliefs   94

Unconditional worth   99

Survival strategies   103

Compensating behaviours   108

The imposter belief   114

6 **Free Your Mind**   **117**

Amygdala key   118

Changing emotion-memories   122

Gone for good   143

7 **Join The Dots**   **145**

Neurochemical secrets   146

The neurochemical dance   150

Change conditional worth   153

Develop unconditional worth   157

Close the loop   166

8 **Worth-based Leadership** **169**

Understanding your team 171

Managing survival strategies 177

Unconditional worth principles 181

9 **Beyond Imposter Syndrome** **185**

The ripple effects 187

Resources **199**

Notes **201**

Acknowledgements **207**

The Author **209**

Introduction

In the late 1400s, Europeans started voyaging across the world's vast oceans, but long-distance sailing involved huge risk. Scurvy – a deadly lack of vitamin C – meant a captain might see half of their crew die by the time the voyage was over. At that time, no one knew about vitamin C, so the cause of scurvy was a mystery.

In 1622, explorer Sir Richard Hawkins found that 'sower lemons and oranges' helped guard against the deadly disease.[1] But it wasn't until 1747 that Dr James Lind successfully trialled lemon juice as a cure. Finally, in 1795, the British Navy started supplying lemons to all their ships, ending scurvy for good. Tragically, in the nearly 200 years between the discovery of the cure and its implementation, over two million sailors died from scurvy, all completely unnecessarily.

Why did it take so long between identifying the cure for scurvy and acting on it?

The reason appears to be that there were too many competing theories and approaches – it was a 'noisy' discussion. History is repeating in the twenty-first century, this time regarding imposter syndrome.

Unlike scurvy, imposter syndrome is not causing millions of deaths, but like scurvy, it creates huge, unnecessary suffering. It causes massive stress and sleepless nights, and leads to impulsivity, poor decision making and emotional reactivity that poisons relationships at work and at home. The stress is implicated in chronic health conditions, and it can lead to burnout, causing talented people to quit successful careers. Furthermore, imposter syndrome has been linked to suicidal thoughts.[2] It is destructive to careers, home life, health and happiness.

The 'cure' for imposter syndrome was actually discovered back in the 1950s by Dr Carl Rogers,[3] but neuroscience (the study of the brain) was in its infancy. At that time, it was thought that the adult brain could not be changed, and so this cure was considered unable to help adults.

Imposter syndrome itself was not identified until 1978.[4] Yes – the solution came before we had even spotted the problem. Since its discovery, we've experienced a similar situation to the great scurvy debate with the noise of multiple theories, no real consensus and too many ineffective approaches. All the while, over 70% of high achievers continue to suffer unnecessarily from imposter syndrome and the fallout it creates, disrupting millions of careers and lives.[5]

A shocking 2020 meta-study of imposter syndrome research found that there were 'no validated treatments for imposter syndrome', despite over forty years of research.[6]

I've written *Outsmart Imposter Syndrome* to reveal a 'cure' using a radical and validated approach that eliminates the root cause of imposter syndrome. In this book, I describe step-by-step how to outsmart and then eliminate imposter syndrome, not just how the process works, but also the research that shows why it works so well.

It's already been seventy years since the root cause of imposter syndrome was discovered. It's time to cut through the noise as you now hold a proven solution in your hands (or on your screen).[7]

Discoveries

My PhD was in engineering rather than psychology, my first choice, but it gave me a taste for research. While I enjoyed engineering, I was more fascinated with the way people operate and practical ways to help them.

After ten years in engineering, I jumped back into psychology / therapy in 2001. Once qualified as a holistic therapist, I started helping clients with all sorts of difficulties. I thoroughly enjoyed the work, but there was a problem. A few clients kept coming back, despite my goal to empower them to move on with the tools to live happier lives.

The burning question for me was: why did these clients keep coming back?

Searching for patterns, I discovered that these clients held certain beliefs that kept them stuck. My work at the time didn't involve beliefs, so naturally I had to explore them.

I came across a powerful coaching approach that changes a fundamental belief that holds people back: conditional worth (that your worth as a human depends on what you do). I experienced this coaching myself and was inspired to train as an Unconditional Worth Coach. The results for me and my clients were transformational, creating deep self-acceptance and calm resilience.

In 2016, one client asked me about imposter syndrome. I looked into it and was astounded: the symptoms of imposter syndrome were an *exact* match for the belief in conditional worth.

Back in research mode, I scoured the academic lit-
erature on imposter syndrome to understand the
symptoms and the effects. Researchers, I discovered, had been trying to match it with personality
traits for nearly forty years and had eventually
concluded that it was *not* a personality trait or a
character flaw.[8]

Further reading uncovered myths and misconceptions
that had popped up about imposter syndrome. Myths
such as it's a women's issue or a beginners' problem,
or even that there is no solution to it. However, I had
already been trained in the solution and I had a strong
suspicion I knew the root cause.

I went on to interview people with imposter syndrome
to verify my conclusion, and the research backed it
up: *The root cause of imposter syndrome is an unconscious
belief in conditional worth.*

I immediately started working exclusively with clients who had imposter syndrome and consistently
got excellent results. Then, as part of my own personal development, I did a week-long neurofeedback
intensive. This is where brain activity is tracked using
electroencephalography (EEG) while going through a
series of exercises to improve brain function.[9] I was so
impressed with the results that I qualified to teach this
neurofeedback work myself.

As a trainer, I needed to explain to participants what
was happening and why the neurofeedback was so

impactful, so I turned once more to research papers on neuroscience and the brain. I was astounded. Again.

I learned how the brain creates and uses beliefs. I also discovered why the unconditional worth coaching works so well and why the neurofeedback process is so effective for changing beliefs.

Finding that some parts of these belief-change processes had strong support in neuroscience research but other parts had no evidence of effectiveness, I pared down my work with clients to only what was proven to work and added in other processes such as neuroregulation, the Polyvagal Model[10] and some high-performance coaching methods. I set it all in the context of imposter syndrome – because imposter syndrome is how conditional worth is experienced by high achievers.

The result was Inner Success, a phenomenally effective one-to-one programme which changes the belief that drives imposter syndrome and eliminates it for good using a systematic step-by-step process. It consistently created remarkable transformation for my clients, instilling effortless confidence, calm, and deep self-acceptance that replaces previously chronic self-doubt.

Excited, I felt a little like the scientists who discovered that lemon juice cures scurvy. Although in my case, my work was standing on the shoulders of research giants in psychology, neuroscience, trauma therapy, physiology and high-performance coaching. Just like the seventeenth-century scientists, I feel frustrated by the noise of the debate. I would hate to see talented individuals suffer needlessly for another thirty years, lost amongst the noisy chaos of unproven theories and myths. This is why I have written *Outsmart Imposter Syndrome.*

The roadmap

What does it mean to *outsmart* imposter syndrome?

Outsmart – to defeat by being *clever* and *cunning*

Clever – being quick to understand, learn and devise or apply ideas

Cunning – having skill in achieving one's ends by being quick-thinking, strategic and ingenious

That is, to outsmart imposter syndrome is to understand it, have the right tools to defeat it and to use them strategically.

In the pages of *Outsmart Imposter Syndrome,* I describe the complete process to eliminate it and why it works so well. I've included the science and theories behind the process, and the real-life transformations I've witnessed with my clients.

To keep these transformations confidential, I have changed details such as name, job, industry, gender, location etc. I've added further anonymity by only using situations I've seen time and again with my clients.

This is not a book for academics (sorry, academics). Indeed, I've simplified some explanations to make them easily understandable for people who aren't researchers and to ensure that the book does not end up three times longer, but I have included references in case you want to dive deeper. Also, neuroscience research continues to uncover more about the brain's operation and the field is advancing rapidly. I can't wait to see what new discoveries will be next!

Outsmart Imposter Syndrome is written for high performers in the business world, established and aspiring leaders, independent consultants and entrepreneurs, as well as anyone aiming for the top of their field or who are in the public eye. This is where imposter syndrome stands out the most and has the most damaging impact. If you're asking yourself whether you are *really* a high achiever despite doing well, then that could well be imposter syndrome, so this book is definitely for you.

In early 2023, Jacinda Ardern, Prime Minister of New Zealand since 2017, resigned because she 'no longer had enough in the tank'.[11] In other words, she'd reached burnout. Three years earlier, she'd revealed that she had imposter syndrome.[12] This link between imposter syndrome and burnout is becoming more well established.[13]

To me, this is an absolute tragedy, as she would have had years of political contribution ahead of her. Whatever you think of her political opinions and policies, no one should have to suffer leaving their job due to burnout.

Had Jacinda Ardern quit due to personal preference, wanting to pursue other dreams or deciding her contribution had been enough, all would have been understandable. However, to see even one person driven to quit because they are overwhelmed and exhausted is heart-breaking for me. Yet I see it again and again. Talented, smart, capable people who are beaten down by imposter syndrome, even though a complete solution for it exists. The pain and turmoil of burnout are absolutely unnecessary suffering.

In 2018, I published the Amazon #1 best-selling book *Unmasking: The coach's guide to imposter syndrome*,[14] to help coaches bring relief to clients suffering from this. With *Outsmart Imposter Syndrome*, this book is for you to look at your own patterns.

Outsmart Imposter Syndrome follows the exact sequence of the Inner Success Method™ I use with clients. It's a momentum process. Like a rolling snowball, a little gets added with each push until you end up with a sturdy solution that has a massive impact. I recommend you read it in the order it's laid out because I explain the science behind each step.

Chapters 2, 3 and 4 cover the essentials of dialling down the stress and calming the symptoms of imposter syndrome. You can comfortably do this by yourself; indeed, this is the basis of my online workshop-style course, also called Outsmart Imposter Syndrome.

Once you've calmed the symptoms, then you're ready to eliminate the root cause. Chapters 5 to 7 take you step-by-step through the radical new approach that is the secret to eliminating imposter syndrome. While it is possible to do this by yourself, I do recommend working with someone able to guide you.

When you make this change, the way you lead and interact with others improves profoundly, which we explore in Chapter 8. Finally, in Chapter 9, we look at what then unfolds beyond your focus on imposter syndrome.

The process in this book is not just theory, and you can absolutely achieve great results for yourself. You can take a free quiz at www.outsmartimpostersyndrome. com/quiz to see how imposter syndrome is impacting you. Further resources for managing and eliminating imposter syndrome are given at the end of the book.

The process described here gets huge, transformational results: freedom from imposter syndrome. While it is therapeutic, though, it is not therapy. It is not to be used as a substitute for good medical or psychological care. If you have a diagnosis of trauma, post-traumatic stress disorder (PTSD) or mental illness, then this work is not for you. You require more personal support than a book and I encourage you to get the medical or psychological care that you need and deserve.

If knowledge is power, then this book is a rocket ship that will take you to the stars. Whether you walk this path by yourself or have a guide for the journey, the result will be a remarkable, positive transformation that stays with you forever.

It is my hope that you will find *Outsmart Imposter Syndrome* easy to read and understand, and that it will give you insight, hope and inspiration. Imposter syndrome is not you, you're not alone and you *can* do something about it.

ONE

The Reality Of Imposter Syndrome

'It doesn't make sense!' blurted James, his forehead creased in frustration. 'I know that I'm doing well, I have plenty of proof, so why am I on edge? I even doubt my decisions now. I'm waking up at night convinced someone's going to catch me out tomorrow, and that they'll fire me for being a Peter.'

I nodded at his sideways reference to the 'Peter Principle',[15] that people get promoted to their level of incompetence. But James wasn't incompetent, far from it. He was Chief Information Officer for a multinational online services company, with three years of outstanding performance reviews behind him, as well as industry awards and press articles full of praise for his innovation and leadership.

Instead of feeling proud and enjoying his evident success, however, James felt stressed, isolated and confused by the disparity. He felt like he was fooling everyone and it was only a matter of time before he got caught.

This definitely sounded like imposter syndrome: an apparent loss of confidence that strikes successful professionals and entrepreneurs, causing you to feel like a fraud when you're not.

'Who have you told about this?' I asked mildly.

'Just you,' he replied. 'I haven't even told my wife.'

Keeping your feelings and concerns a secret is a common behaviour pattern with imposter syndrome. Of course, you're worried that if anyone were to find out that you are the 'fraud' you believe yourself to be, then the consequences would be dire.

This secrecy is a trap. You don't tell anyone because you think that only you feel this way, and that maybe you don't really belong in your career, profession, role etc. However, if everyone keeps their imposter feelings a secret, then everyone thinks that it's just them. This can lead to a lot of stress, isolation and a deep sense of not belonging.

'What if I told you that seven out of ten high achievers experience imposter syndrome at some point in their careers?' I said.

James looked sceptical. 'Surely I would have noticed that? My colleagues are an impressive bunch, and everyone else seems to be doing so well.'

'Yes, that's because you're comparing how well they seem to be doing on the outside to how you're feeling on the inside,' I pointed out. 'It's an invalid comparison. Of course, if they keep their imposter syndrome a secret, just like you do, you wouldn't have seen it. Do your colleagues praise you for your work and achievements?'

'I do get recognition, but I think they're exaggerating. Or they want something,' James said with a flicker of mistrust. 'I've just been lucky. Good timing, extra help and a great team. Anyone could have done it, so I usually change the subject.'

Here, James is deflecting the praise. Not because he's being modest or humble, but because he genuinely believes that anyone could have achieved what he has.

'And have you been thinking about getting more qualifications recently?' I asked.

'Yes, I have,' he said, surprised. 'There's another programme at the business school where I earned my MBA. My wife's been teasing me about having so many letters after my name.'

Another self-judgement with imposter syndrome is wanting more of something to counter the feeling of not being good enough. For example, you think you don't have enough qualifications, money, companies or material possessions, even when you have a lot. No matter how much you attain, there is a continued desire for more, as if having more could prove to you that you are not a fraud. One clue to this imposter behaviour is that when you get stressed, your 'solution' is to get another qualification.

James jumped up and started pacing, clearly annoyed with himself for seeing no viable solution to his problem.

'Is the conclusion you make,' I said, watching James slowly sit down again, 'that it must be you? That maybe there's something wrong with you? Maybe you're not good enough?' James just nodded, looking glum.

Does this sound a bit like you? If it does, it's not surprising because as I told James, seven out of ten high achievers experience imposter syndrome at some point in their career. You may see yourself in some of James's feelings and behaviours, although to a different degree. Everybody has their own combination of such behaviours. Or you may simply doubt yourself or doubt that you're good enough to be at the level you've already reached.

A key problem of imposter syndrome is the confusion that it causes. Logically and intellectually, you know that you're competent. You are successful, having had promotions, great reviews or even awards, but internally, you don't feel like 'a success'. All you notice is how much of a struggle your work life is.

This contrast between your outward success and your internal feelings is a puzzle for your mind. Your mind doesn't like puzzles (uncertainty), but it does like *solving* them. To solve this puzzle, it falsely concludes that 'It must be me. Maybe I'm not as good as everyone else seems to think I am. I must be a fraud. I hope they don't find out!' Unfortunately, this reinforces the negative imposter syndrome thinking and drives a continuous cycle of these symptoms.

Outsmart Imposter Syndrome resolves this puzzling contrast and removes confusion, showing you how to break free from the unnecessary suffering of imposter syndrome. Suffering that has the potential to ruin your career, your health and your life.

Now we'll look at the reality of imposter syndrome, its symptoms, who gets it and the impact it can have.

What is imposter syndrome?

Imposter syndrome is not technically a syndrome as defined by medical professionals. It does not appear in the *Diagnostic and Statistical Manual of Mental Disorders*, and a doctor or a psychologist will not diagnose you with it.

This is why some professionals say imposter syndrome doesn't exist, as it is not an official medical syndrome. However, the experience of imposter syndrome is very real.

When Drs Pauline Clance and Suzanne Imes first identified it as an observed pattern of thought and behaviour in 1978, they called it the imposter phenomenon. I suspect people started calling it imposter syndrome because it's a catchier name and 'syndrome' is easier to pronounce. The term has stuck and 'imposter syndrome' it is.

However, it is reassuring that imposter syndrome does not require medication, surgery or psychotherapy. You're not in any way defective or broken, which is something people sometimes fear. Indeed, while psychotherapy takes people from mental dysfunction to normal functioning, imposter syndrome *is* normal functioning, albeit leaning into more negative emotions than positive, and no therapy is required.

We first need to define imposter syndrome:

> Imposter syndrome is *self-doubt, the secret feeling of being a fraud when you're not, and the fear of being found out.*

With imposter syndrome, you assume that you've fooled everyone into thinking you're better than you are. It holds you back from achieving what you're truly capable of and from enjoying the satisfaction of your success. When you resolve the confusion, understand what's going on and know what you can do about it, then you will find a greater sense of peace.

Who gets imposter syndrome?

Even though 30% of people report not having imposter syndrome, it doesn't mean that they don't have it. Most of that 30% have found ways to manage the symptoms well without being aware that they do so. Others are unobservant, and some flat-out deny that they have any problems because to acknowledge this would feel like a failure in itself. Finally, 4% of high achievers in business show sociopathic/psychopathic behavioural and thinking patterns,[16] which means their brains don't recognise fear in the way healthy brains would.

This suggests that the percentage of people struck by imposter syndrome is likely much higher than 70%. Hopefully, this figure will help reassure you that it's not 'just you'.

The issue of gender and imposter syndrome surfaces regularly too. The first research into the phenomenon by Clance and Imes focused on female graduate students. Many studies after that seemed to confirm that women experience it more than men, suggesting imposter syndrome was mainly a women's problem. But in 1997, the surveys were repeated using a different method.[17] Was there an unidentified social bias going on?

The answer is yes. The surveys had not been 100% anonymous. When participants trusted Dr Sharon Fried-Buchalter's survey to be completely anonymous, she found that men experience imposter syndrome in the same numbers as women. The social bias captured in previous studies was that men are traditionally discouraged from revealing a perceived weakness, and many did not feel comfortable doing so unless the survey was completely anonymous.

This mistaken gender difference is damaging to everyone. It wrongly implies that women are inherently flawed, or it makes them think they are, which feeds into the imposter feeling. Thinking of it as a 'women's issue' causes those men who experience imposter syndrome to feel even more isolated, that they too are intrinsically flawed and don't belong.

Despite this finding being nearly thirty years old, I still see many people quoting old research and claiming there is a gender difference, and new studies being performed without the necessary anonymity.

Impact of imposter syndrome

Imposter syndrome creates confusion, isolation, anxiety, overwhelm and exhaustion. It can lead to you quitting your job or even your whole career.

The huge stress it creates is distracting. You lose focus and clarity, struggle to make sound decisions, lose productivity and spend long hours overworking just to keep up. Worst of all, you think that these behaviours and stress levels are your fault, a result of some kind of character flaw or weakness. This means you don't think that there's anything you can do about it, except hide it and hope nobody finds out.

Few people realise that they are suffering with imposter syndrome, and instead assume it is an inherent flaw in themselves. Even fewer realise that there could be a solution to this problem.

Imposter syndrome has a greater influence than just affecting your internal thoughts, feelings and reactions. Its impact spreads like a ripple in a pond. It affects how you interact with your colleagues and your team, leading to poor communication, reduced productivity and creativity, and increased stress all round.

It impacts your ability to switch off and be present with your family and eats into the time you spend with them, too. I've even seen the tension this creates lead directly to relationship breakdown and divorce.

At the highest level, imposter syndrome gets in the way of your contribution to your company, your community and humankind.

Some people assert that imposter syndrome is a superpower. That is, the stress and anxiety that imposter syndrome causes are somehow proof that you care deeply about your work, or are just dealing with 'growing pains'. They suggest you should embrace the discomfort and soldier on. I don't find this helpful.

This is like trying to walk with a nail in your shoe. Every step is slow, painful and difficult. Instead of embracing this pain to prove that you're tough, let's simply remove the nail and allow you to walk pain-free, and then you will naturally be at your best without unnecessary hindrance and suffering.

Imposter syndrome symptoms

Imposter syndrome is comprised of the symptoms that you see and the root cause that you don't see. Most people only notice imposter syndrome indirectly from their stress levels and symptoms, which is confusing because the cause is not obvious. They can't see why 'stress' or 'beliefs' could possibly have such a big impact on their life and career, or why they should cause so much disruption and distress. Let's look at the imposter syndrome symptoms to get a full picture of the experience.

The visible symptoms can be divided into three types:

1. Imposter syndrome thoughts

2. Physiological stress

3. Imposter syndrome behaviours

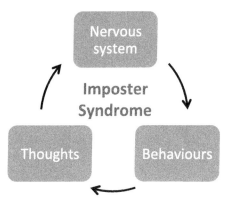

Imposter syndrome thoughts include self-doubt, feeling not good enough, worrying about being found out to be a fraud (even though you're not). Over-thinking and rumination like this send stress signals to your brain and your body responds by creating tension, anxiety and overwhelm.

To alleviate this physiological and emotional stress, you unwittingly resort to coping behaviours characteristic of imposter syndrome. These include procrastination, comparing, over-preparing and perfectionism.

However, these behaviours are distracting and unproductive. You criticise or judge yourself for doing them because you know they are holding you back or dragging you down. This self-judgement then reinforces the imposter syndrome thoughts.

It is a cycle that continually feeds into itself. It is a complex issue, which explains why the myth has arisen that there is no way to resolve it.

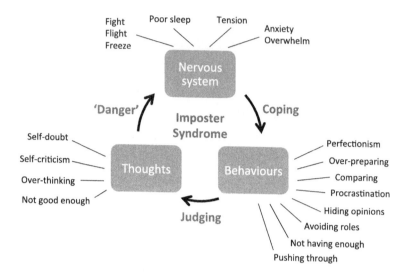

Some people try to fix imposter syndrome by focusing on one type of symptom. For example, they experiment with mindset and affirmations for the imposter thinking, or they try habit change techniques for the behaviours. Despite being useful techniques for other situations, this one-symptom approach has only limited success for imposter syndrome because you need to break the complete cycle. That is, you need to tackle all three symptoms simultaneously. When you do, you will start to feel lighter, calmer and more in control than you have in a long time.

The symptoms are not the real problem here, they are just what you can see. Once you have dialled down the symptoms, then you are ready to tackle the root cause of imposter syndrome and eliminate it for good.

Real solutions

With imposter syndrome, you know intellectually that you are capable and competent, but at the same time you have a sneaking suspicion that you're not *quite* good enough. You ignore the evidence of your successes because they never seem to prove to yourself that you *are* good enough.

Holding these two opposing views at the same time is confusing. As a logical, rational person, you try and figure out why you don't believe in yourself, but addressing this confusion at the level of conscious thought won't work because it's not an intellectual issue. There are emotional and physiological factors, of which you may not be aware.

To outsmart imposter syndrome, we need to calm the symptoms, and then remove the root cause. We start with how to calm the physiological stress symptoms that affect the nervous system.

Ready? Let's begin.

TWO
Still The Storm

In 2013, researchers at the ESADE Business School in Spain conducted a remarkable experiment.[18] They wired up MBA students to sensors to measure their physical and mental activity, then had them work through a case study as a group. The researchers filmed all the interactions and documented how the students solved the problem. They were searching for clues to what makes an outstanding or transformational leader.

Their conclusion was not what you might expect. The outstanding leaders in this experiment were not those who talked the most or who had the best ideas. The outstanding leaders were the ones who could best regulate their nervous system. That is, the ones who could remain calm, creative and open-minded throughout.

The study demonstrated that neuroregulation is an essential skill for good leadership. Unfortunately, imposter syndrome is a prime disruptor of neuro-regulation. It makes it hard for you to stay calm and therefore impacts your leadership performance.

This physiological symptom of imposter syndrome has a dramatic negative impact not just on your leadership, but also on your energy, health, mood, performance, productivity, and focus, and your enjoyment and satisfaction at work. For this reason, learning to regulate your nervous system is the first step in outsmarting imposter syndrome.

In this chapter, we'll explore the physiological stress symptom, what it looks like and how you can manage it.

Activated nervous system

When faced with life-threatening danger, our nervous system gets activated and goes into one of three defensive states: fight, flight or freeze.[19] This normal, natural response to potential danger is a fundamental survival mechanism without which you and I wouldn't be here because our ancestors would have died out many thousands of years ago.

Let's take a look at each state in detail, seeing how a neurological response that was essential to our ancestors might not serve us so well in the modern world.

Fight state

Rewind about 50,000 years to Palaeolithic times. Brac is physiologically a modern human, but his everyday life is vastly different from our twenty-first century one.

Walking through the sub-tropical rainforest, Brac comes across a small troop of baboons. The startled baboons advance aggressively, shrieking and baring their sharp teeth. Together, they could seriously injure or kill Brac.

Brac responds immediately. He grabs a small fallen branch and swings it towards the advancing monkeys. Standing up as tall as he can, he roars at them. The baboons back off quickly and dash into the undergrowth. Brac continues to shout at them and wave the branch around even after they've been driven off. Panting, he then slowly calms down again.

Brac's nervous system had immediately gone into the fight state when he saw that he might be attacked. Fight is a defensive nervous system state, driving you to attack to protect yourself and survive a threat. Physically, you feel heat that you might describe as a 'fire in your belly'. You might feel your cheeks going red, notice muscle tension, clench your fists or your jaw, all accompanied by a racing heart and increased blood pressure.

Stress hormones of cortisol and adrenaline are released into your bloodstream to help your muscles react quickly in your defence. The related emotions are anger and irritation, and you may be more emotionally reactive than usual. In this state, you might lash out physically, or want to, although in modern times, you're more likely to lash out verbally or intimidate others. You might say things that you don't mean, blurting out personal attacks and low blows.

Kim, Chief Executive Officer (CEO) of a Fintech company, recognised right away that her go-to nervous system state was fight. When challenged, she would become defensive, and then try to intimidate people and be aggressive towards them. She was unyielding when she thought people had done her wrong, and even had a list of 'enemies', those she'd had a conflict with and would never forgive. She would escalate, argue, then burn bridges and torch relationships.

This behaviour was costing her dearly, both personally and professionally. It made her tough to work with, and she knew that she had lost friends, support and opportunities in the past because of it. Kim recognised how much this pattern was hurting her, not only her career, but also her industry influence, which in turn directly affected the company. It stopped her from being as effective, and therefore as successful, as she could have been.

To compound her frustration, she seemed unable to break the pattern. Kim's automatic angry reactions felt like they were outside of her control.

Flight state

Brac takes a short break after his encounter with the baboons, then continues along the forest trail. He hears a rustle and catches sight of a smooth black shape slithering through the undergrowth. Brac leaps back immediately, and then takes several rapid steps away, his eyes fixed on that shape.

Soon enough, a large black snake slides across the muddy path. Brac recognises that it's a poisonous snake whose bite could be fatal. His heart is racing and again he's breathing hard.

The flight state is the urge to run away or avoid things. Brac acts fast, not because he's thought about the situation, but because his body and nervous system reacted automatically. This instinctive reaction keeps him alive, which is more than can be said for his brother, Yun, who died from a snake bite as a teenager. If Yun had had faster reflexes, he might have lived.

In the flight state, you literally want to run away or disappear. You might feel this state physically as cold hands and feet, a racing heart, shakiness in your limbs or a buzzing in your belly. Again, stress hormones are released into the bloodstream to help ready you for escape. The emotions of flight are anxiety and trepidation.

Modern versions of flight can be avoiding people or situations, not wanting to go to work in the morning, or withdrawing in situations where you can't physically leave. It can lead to you simply quitting, which can affect all areas of life including your family, your job and your community.

Hannah, the Chief Product Officer (CPO) at an international cyber-security firm, was due to deliver a high-stakes presentation to an important client. She'd done this many times before, but something seemed different this time. She procrastinated in creating the presentation, then spent long hours over-preparing, and she worried about it for weeks.

She became more stressed and exhausted as the meeting drew nearer. Just three days before it, she marched into her CEO's office, quit her job and left the same day.

Hannah was not thinking at all about career planning, financial commitments or family repercussions. She was purely reacting to her overwhelming stress. Her nervous system was driving her to run away. Her CEO was mystified because he had consistently praised Hannah for the great job she was doing and had no idea that she was so stressed.

Freeze state

Shaken and wary, Brac carries on through the forest, looking carefully around for more dangers. He hears the deep, low growl of a tiger nearby. Brac immediately freezes. He doesn't move and holds his breath.

Like all cats, the tiger's attention is drawn to sudden movements and noises. By freezing completely, Brac might just escape the tiger's notice.

He stays where he is for quite some time, motionless, with just his eyes scanning the forest around him, his ears listening out for any more signs of the tiger. The tiger had been stalking a deer, and after Brac freezes, it resumes its original hunt.

After what seems like an age rooted to the spot, Brac hears the tiger chase the deer some distance away. Slowly, Brac starts to move again before hurrying away in the opposite direction as quickly and quietly as he can.

The freeze state is the 'rabbit in the headlights' moment. You feel stuck and hold your breath. Your muscles may seem weak and difficult to move. You might feel nausea, loss of appetite or brain fog. Your mind might go blank and you may not be able to remember key facts and figures. Emotionally, freeze can feel like overwhelm, numbness or panic.

James was in a boardroom meeting when the chairman suddenly turned on him, blaming him for recent poor results, loudly and aggressively. James was used to passionate outbursts in top-level meetings, he saw it as going with the territory, but this time, he was stunned. Not only because it was unjustified, but more so because the chairman had always been a supporter and mentor to James, so it was a total shock.

33

His mind went blank, he felt sick and he couldn't speak or move for what seemed like an age. Finally, he excused himself and went to the bathroom to splash water on his face.

What had just happened? James had never experienced this before and was as shocked by his own response as by the chairman's sudden attack. James's nervous system had, in fact, gone into the freeze state.

Do you recognise any or all of these nervous system states? All of them have an out-of-control feel to them, which makes sense because you're not in control. The nervous system states get triggered automatically by signs of a threat. Your physiology takes over, correctly so as it's working to preserve your life, like it did for Brac. He may have felt a little foolish if, on his way home, he'd jumped back quickly at another snake, only to realise that it was an old tree root, but it was better for his nervous system to be over-active rather than under-active, which could cost him his life. These ancient survival mechanisms echo down the ages and are still fully functional in our bodies today.

However, this response isn't helpful in the modern world where we rarely face a life-threatening situation. You may have a clear recollection of one big incident triggering fight, flight or freeze, or you may notice a repeating pattern and find yourself in these states again and again. This physiological stress is distinct from thought-based stresses such as worry or regret.

Cost of nervous system activation

When your system goes into the fight or flight state, the blood flow in your body changes. Extra blood is diverted to the muscles, readying them for fighting or running away.

This blood is taken from the peripheries of your body, your digestive system and the prefrontal cortex in the brain, which is the logical thinking and strategic planning region that lies just behind your forehead. With a reduced blood flow, your prefrontal cortex literally does not have the resources, the oxygen and the nutrients that it needs to make good decisions and control emotional reactivity. Your thinking becomes foggy, you are distracted, lose clarity, and your scope of creative thought narrows. You are unable to perform at your best when your body is stressed in this high-alert state.[20]

A 2012 Princeton University study found that a person's intelligence quotient (IQ) is temporarily reduced by an average of thirteen points when they're in this state.[21] Typical IQ lies between 75 and 125, so thirteen IQ points is a lot of smarts for anyone to lose access to!

When you're in the fight, flight or freeze state, your brain is actively looking out for dangerous situations and views even neutral events as potential threats. That is, you will be more wary, hostile, untrusting and suspicious. You feel like you are out of control with an activated nervous system, and you realise it's detrimental to you, your work and your relationships. You might conclude there must be something 'wrong' with you. It undermines your confidence, increases self-doubt and reinforces the imposter syndrome thinking that maybe you're not good enough after all.

Continual high stress levels change the chemical and hormonal signalling in your body, create stress-related illness, lower your immune response and contribute to the major chronic disorders of our time, such as atherosclerosis, heart disease, diabetes and cancer.[22] Many people take antidepressants or medications for stress, anxiety and sleep issues in an attempt to regulate this chronic nervous system activation.[23]

Alternatively, they 'self-medicate' with alcohol, drugs, food and other addictive escapes. Indeed, the top 20% income bracket has a higher proportion of alcoholics than the rest of the population.[24] This suggests high levels of stress accompany the highest levels of achievement.

Polyvagal Model

These dramatic changes in your physiology can be explained by the Polyvagal Model of the nervous system. The vagus nerve, which is actually three interconnecting nerves, links the brain to the body.

It carries instructions for fight, flight and freeze to the rest of the body in moments of perceived threat.

The command to shift from one state to another comes from two small almond-sized parts of the brain (jointly) called the amygdala. The amygdala filters incoming sensory data, looking out for matches to scenarios it would label as dangerous. In the case of our caveman ancestors, such dangers would be a troop of baboons, a snake hidden in the grass or a prowling tiger.

To take a modern-day analogy, the amygdala is like a computer virus checker that searches your email for dangerous viruses before they reach your inbox. In the same way, the amygdala checks for dangers that it determines could hurt, damage or kill you.

The amygdala receives information coming up through the brain stem before it reaches the prefrontal cortex. Whatever information the prefrontal cortex receives, the amygdala has checked it first. This means that when your nervous system has been triggered, the information has not yet reached the prefrontal cortex for evaluation or assessment. The amygdala has already reacted. Psychologists call this an amygdala hijack because it has taken over your body without your conscious consent.[25]

Whenever you notice you have been triggered into fight, flight or freeze, you might be tempted to criticise yourself because you're not in control.

However, that is because your logical brain never had the opportunity to think about it or exert conscious control.

Such nervous system activation is a normal, natural part of your body's defences. If you know how to manage and regulate your nervous system, however, then you will be able to stay calm and in control with all your wits about you. With this neuroregulation, you will gain the advantage that the ESADE research showed makes an outstanding leader.

Neuroregulation

The first step to proactively regulating your nervous system and staying calm is to become aware of when it is triggered. Notice which nervous system state your body goes into most often. It will tend to follow a similar pattern most of the time.

If you do nothing when your nervous system gets activated, it could take one hour or more for your liver to filter out the stress hormones and for your system to calm down again.[26] That is a long time to feel you're out of control, emotionally reactive, distracted, not thinking clearly and physically stressed.

Ideally, you need to get out of this activated nervous system state as quickly as possible. Here are a few ways to do this.

Shaking out

To manage this activated state, you can do what animals do when they have stress hormones in their system. Imagine a deer that's just escaped a chasing lion. Once the deer stops running and realises it's safe, its muscles twitch while it is standing still. This is the natural way an animal flushes out the stress hormones from their blood, and it works well when adapted for humans too.[27]

The human version is to shake out the stress hormones. Stand up and start moving your hands as if you're flicking thick mud off them. Do this quite vigorously, making it a big movement using your arms and shoulders. Shake faster while bouncing at the knees. Shake out one leg in the same way, and then the other leg. Next, wiggle your back as if you're a wet dog shaking itself to get dry.

Do all of this for a minute or two until you're breathless. When you stop, you're likely to feel tingling.

Once you've shaken out the stress hormones, do slow, deep breathing to calm your nervous system even more. There's a great breathing technique the special forces use for this, called the box breath.

- Breathe in for a count of four
- Hold for a count of four

- Breathe out for four

- Hold for four

- Cycle round a few times until the tingling has gone away

Next, use your senses to connect you to the environment. That is, look around you and pay close attention to what you see. Look at colours, shapes and different objects. Listen to the sounds around you and try to identify each one. Focus on the sensation of touch by noticing the temperature and texture of surfaces with your fingers. Feel the pressure of the seat or floor wherever it touches your body. Cross your arms and stroke yourself from shoulder to elbow like you would pet an animal. By deliberately reconnecting your senses to your environment in this way, you quickly get your nervous system even calmer.

Shaking out like this is excellent when you are in the fight or flight state. For the freeze state, you need to 'unfreeze' yourself before you can shake out.

To unfreeze, start with the same slow, deep breathing, and then gently move your body slowly. Stretch and splay your fingers and toes. Then spread this movement to your arms and legs with long, slow stretches. Stand to stretch and twist your torso. If you find yourself yawning, go with it and make it a big yawn. Wake up a frozen voice by humming long notes, all the while maintaining steady, deep breathing.

At this point, if you feel a bit tingly, energised or anxious, you can do the shaking out process. If not, you can skip straight to connecting your senses to the space around you.

You now have several powerful techniques to regulate your nervous system quickly. Use them whenever you notice your nervous system has been activated. Also use them if you are about to go into a stressful situation to get yourself as calm as possible beforehand.

Maintain calm

When people get stressed, everything can suddenly feel urgent and time-pressured. They often stop doing the things that are good for them, because self-care appears to be less important in the face of immediate demands on their time and energy. However, at times like these, it is even more important to get calm and stay calm.

To do this, list the things that you already know relax you. It could be that you enjoy reading or listening to music. You may like to meditate. It could be that you love dancing, and indeed any exercise, even a walk around the neighbourhood, is a great way to help calm your body.

Look at which social events relax you. Decide whether you prefer spending time in a group, with just one person or alone. Seek out community, support, activity and social groups for more connection.

Singing is a wonderful way to relax as it also gets you breathing rhythmically. If you do this in a community environment such as a choir or karaoke, the social connection enhances its positive effects.

Music can have a profound influence on your physiology too. It's likely you already know which music makes you feel good. Create a playlist of songs that specifically influence your nervous system state in a positive way.

Build your neuroregulation maintenance plan comprising everything that calms you and schedule it into a regular routine. This solid foundation continually brings you back to a calm state and allows you to stay that way for longer.

The fellow state

There is another nervous system state identified by the Polyvagal Model: the social-engagement state or, as I call it, the fellow state.[28] The fellow state is the default human nervous system state when we are *not* feeling under threat, because humans are social beings wired to cooperate and survive together in a community.

When you go from stressed back to the fellow state, you regain access to your full mental capacity as normal blood flow is returned to your brain's prefrontal cortex. You naturally feel cooperative, safe, open and creative. You're able to think clearly. Emotionally, you feel calm and enjoy things more. You laugh more easily and feel physically relaxed.

Your brain also takes cues from others as to whether danger lurks nearby or not. The nervous systems of the people around you can communicate safety (ie no danger) and acceptance. If they're relaxed and feeling safe, then it helps you to relax and feel safe, so talking with somebody supportive and making eye contact is a great help to get into the fellow state too.

Regulate yourself

The neuroregulation tools of shaking out and maintaining calm mean that you can regulate your nervous system whenever you need to, becoming more in control, more productive, more focused and more creative than before. You will be able to think clearly and make good decisions by virtue of being in the fellow state.

It's important to remember that an activated nervous system is a normal process that has been triggered by a perceived threat. It is *not* your personality, a weakness or a flaw. This realisation removes a whole layer of self-criticism and helps to stop the cycle of negative thinking from re-triggering the nervous system. Instead of judging your nervous system state, you can see it as an event that happens in your body that you

OUTSMART IMPOSTER SYNDROME

now know how to handle. This alone brings a huge sense of relief as you feel more in control, and you stop the physiological stress symptom from reinforcing the imposter syndrome thoughts of not being good enough, which in turn helps you relax.

You could stop at this point and practising your new awareness and neuroregulation skills, you would gradually make your life calmer and more stable, but we have a lot further to go with more gains to be won.

As you witness your nervous system response, you might get curious as to why your nervous system has been triggered in the first place. If you knew exactly what triggered your amygdala, then you could make plans to manage your environment so that you'd get triggered less.

This is another big step to dialling down imposter syndrome. We'll look at managing your external environment in detail next.

THREE

Calm Imposter Triggers

James would happily give a talk to 1,000 people in a big company meeting, but he would get anxious about presenting to the twelve people in the board meeting. His colleague, René, was the exact opposite and found that the larger the audience, the higher the stress levels.

Although this was a standing joke between them, it illustrates how personal and individual your imposter syndrome experience is. Imposter feelings can come and go depending on the situation, but when you can identify triggers in your environment that set off your nervous system, then you are able to create a proactive plan to manage them.

Certain activities activate your nervous system because your amygdala has considered them a threat, as we saw in the previous chapter. This is how your system is supposed to work if the danger were a real threat, and it's how human physiology has always worked. Our ancient ancestors didn't encounter tigers and snakes every day (or at least, we hope they didn't). Instead, it'd be occasional, but the nervous system was always primed to react.

Our modern world is so different from our ancestors' times. We live in a fast-paced world, with long work hours and often little to no proximity to nature. We experience events that activate our nervous system far more frequently, even though there is rarely real danger present. This repeated physiological stress drives imposter behaviours, which we'll cover in the next chapter, and reinforces imposter syndrome thoughts, so the cycle of symptoms continues. So that we can remain calm and in control as much as possible, our next step is to manage the external imposter syndrome triggers.

There are two typical environment triggers for the nervous system. The first is a specific 'imposter activity' and the second relates to the combination of high challenge with low support.

Imposter activity

High achievers with imposter syndrome do not have low self-esteem or low confidence. Instead, they are capable, competent people who get things done and make a difference. However, there is often one particular activity that trips them up: their imposter activity.

A promotion or new business opportunity brings more responsibilities, such as financial budgeting, technical oversight, more people management, strategic planning or creative demands, and these expand the scope of your work. Among these new responsibilities, you might discover that there is one activity that, for some mysterious reason, is far more uncomfortable than all the rest.

This explains why imposter syndrome is so common in high achievers. If you were to continue doing the same job year after year, you would not take on new responsibilities, and so you might never encounter a potential imposter activity.

However, imposter syndrome is not caused by being new to something. It is often confused with being a beginner, attempting new things or having a lack of skill. But this is simply the discomfort many people feel in the process of learning. If you feel uncomfortable because you don't have experience in a new area, the solution is to get some good training appropriate to your level. Get the training and you will feel more comfortable.

In contrast, imposter syndrome strikes when you are *already* capable and competent. Then, the fact that the imposter activity is so taxing is not about a lack of skill. You can even excel at something and still get triggered by it. You have a disproportionate level of anxiety around this activity and worry that if you mess it up, then everything will fall apart. Consequently, you can't measure what triggers you by whether you are good or bad at it.

Manage imposter activities

Explore which activities make you feel nervous, worried, overwhelmed, or cause you sleepless nights or significant stress. Once you are aware of the top trigger(s), you can plan for them. If you have, say, three imposter activities, avoid doing them all on the same day wherever possible. In other words, don't group activities that you know will trigger you. Instead, try to space them out through your day and week.

If you've one imposter activity planned, then make sure you've scheduled less stressful events around it. If you schedule imposter activities with the goal of staying calm, then you can regulate your nervous system better. Being calm in turn makes you less susceptible to the imposter activity triggering you in the first place.

Particularly now that many people work from home and many meetings are conducted online, your calendar can easily become full of back-to-back meetings. This does not allow you time to take a break or calm down between them, so your stress can accumulate from meeting to meeting. You become less able to perform at your best and the cumulative stress can build to overwhelm. To counter this, scheduling short breaks between meetings can work wonders.

Furthermore, you can carve out time for regulating your nervous system to a calmer baseline ahead of an imposter activity. If you're about to go into a meeting that you know will be triggering, for example, do everything you can to relax and de-stress before it starts. Use the powerful neuroregulation techniques described in Chapter 2 to achieve this.

Similarly, if you've just had a situation trigger your nervous system, do whatever you can to calm down quickly afterwards to avoid carrying the stress on to the next event. Taking a minute to slow your breathing and relax your muscles can be more helpful than you might expect.

Circumstances

The other major external trigger for imposter syndrome involves situations that combine high levels of challenge with low levels of support. Smart management of imposter syndrome must include tracking and adjusting the amount of challenge and support on an ongoing basis.

Challenge

'Challenge' is a neutral word, neither good nor bad. It can be the adventure of a difficult task and an opportunity to stretch ourselves to see how much we can achieve. When we're calm and clear headed, then a challenge is an exciting experience. There is a possibility of failure, but we're willing to risk that for the chance to prevail.

Challenging ourselves in this way is a natural human desire, driven by an innate urge to adapt ourselves to new and testing situations. When we're inspired to challenge ourselves and we succeed, we get a hit of feel-good chemicals in our brain. We're excited and thrilled with our achievement.

In fact, in high-performance environments, you can reach the flow state, which is effortless, energised, focused, intense and enjoyable. Athletes call it 'the zone', but it is not only seen in sports. You can experience the flow state in your work life as well. A study of this expansive flow state shows that it occurs when you are working at just 4% above your capacity.[29] This smallest of stretches makes high performance so exciting.

However, a challenge can be negative when things become too much – too difficult, overwhelming and exhausting. If the challenge is applied externally and it is beyond your resources to cope with it, it can become even more stressful. Your nervous system gets activated, which reduces your capacity to meet any further challenges. It's easy to see how a positive challenge can turn into a negative one, especially when you're already operating at the edges of your previous experience, even though this edge is where you would feel most rewarded if you did succeed.

An obvious source of unnecessary stress is what I'd call a bad challenge. This can be a toxic work environment, or bullying and difficult people. It can be being under-resourced at work and having more on your plate than you can reasonably accomplish.

However, avoiding big challenges entirely is not the answer. That road will lead us to regret for what we might have otherwise accomplished and feel disappointment in ourselves.

Where is the sweet spot? As shown in the graph above, when the stress levels are too low, it's unsatisfying. You're bored, you're underutilised and it's not an exciting way to live your life for sure.

As demands and challenges increase, your performance improves as you become excited, motivated, energised and focused. It is a beneficial stress, known as eustress.

When the challenge increases further, adding too much stress, your performance starts to decline. Pushing through when you're in a high-challenge situation is a sure-fire way to become burnt out and exhausted. Ironically, this further decreases your performance levels, as we saw in the last chapter.

The arrow on the graph is the point of high performance that is close to burnout. This is why actively managing challenge is a must. Maximising the good challenge and minimising the bad challenge will help keep you in a high-performance state without falling into the distress stage.

Blame

When levels of challenge are high and people get overwhelmed, they can blame themselves and think there's something wrong with them. Maybe, they tell themselves, they're not good enough. This is classic imposter syndrome thinking in response to an overly challenging environment. It can lead to a downward spiral in energy and mood.

A similar mistake can be blaming other people or the job itself for our low energy and mood when the real cause of stress is that we are overwhelmed with workload, and our challenge levels are descending into distress.

Sayid was an executive in one of the 'big four' professional services companies. He was overwhelmed, burnt out and unhappy, despite all his achievements and great performance. He blamed himself and decided that maybe he wasn't cut out for the corporate life.

As a result, he quit and became an independent consultant. His new business grew well, but the feelings of not being good enough didn't go away. Sayid still felt like a fraud. He realised then that the culprit was not his work environment at all, past or present, but imposter syndrome. Once he understood this, Sayid stopped blaming his work or himself and set about solving the real problem, which is imposter syndrome.

Toxic environment

Sometimes, the 'bad challenge' we experience is a toxic workplace. This may be an environment where people actively work against us, are hostile or critical, and may include bullying and intimidation. Not only are they criticising, but they're doing it in an angry, aggressive way. Resentment and even sabotage may be present in the work environment too.

A toxic workplace can also be due to the company culture itself. It can come from any person: a boss, a colleague, our team members, the support staff, suppliers or customers.

First and foremost, if you're in a toxic work environment, seek all the help and support you can find. I also recommend doing what you can to change the dysfunction in the workplace. Report it, talk about it and explore solutions.

If change is not possible, then leaving a toxic environment can be the wisest decision. Feeling trapped in any situation is stressful, but feeling trapped in a toxic environment will likely remain a never-ending cause of stress.

Even when you develop the ability to handle a toxic workplace, changing your work environment may still be a good move. You are worthy of a pleasant and supportive workplace and you always have a choice.

Challenges and the nervous system

Many high achievers use a form of focus called compartmentalisation to deal with stress. Compartmentalisation is shutting out distracting thoughts, feelings and memories and paying attention only to the matter at hand. This is a valuable technique in an emergency where taking fast action is paramount.

Misapplied, however, compartmentalisation becomes unhelpful or destructive. Since it is the active suppression of thoughts and feelings, it is detrimental on a long-term, routine basis, because it does not reduce the levels of stress and discomfort.

Say, for example, you have an argument with your partner that is unresolved before you leave for work one morning. When you get into work, you deliberately compartmentalise it so that you are no longer thinking about the argument and can focus on work. But whether you're aware of it or not, the residual anger or hurt has triggered your nervous system. This will subconsciously colour everything you do, influencing your interactions with the people around you.

If something goes wrong later that day, compartmentalising will cause you to look for the root of the stress at work.[30] If you can't see any cause at work, the mystery can be 'solved' by thinking that maybe it's you. Maybe your qualities or personal characteristics aren't up to the job. This self-doubt about your ability to fulfil your role is imposter syndrome triggered by suppressed stress from home.

Whether the influence is a one-off event, for example an argument, or a repeating stressor like a relationship deteriorating, every experience we have affects and informs every other. We are not different people when we play different roles; we bring our whole selves to all parts of our lives. This is especially true when it comes to nervous system activation, which makes managing challenge essential.

Track challenge

You may not always notice the level of challenge changing unless you pay close attention. A good analogy is if you are an accomplished runner, but you have a sprained ankle. The circumstances have changed, so of course you're not going to be running at your best.

The expectation that we should always deliver the same results regardless of circumstances is unrealistic and ignores the influence of the environment around us. Underlying this is the fear of making a mistake, not being good enough or doing something wrong, that is, imposter syndrome thinking.

We want to be able to deliver consistent high performance and achieve our best every day. But we only get that by tracking and balancing our challenge and support on a continual, responsive basis.

Manage all challenges

Stress is cumulative, regardless of the source. There will be events and challenges outside of work that add to your overall stress, which later impacts your performance at work. Managing your challenges well means reducing the unnecessary ones in *every* area of your life, leaving you fully able to meet the good, exciting ones with energy and relish.

Look to reduce challenge in areas such as work, relationships, finances, logistics such as household chores and taking the kids to school, dependents, your health, hobbies, and one-off events. Consider each area of your life and see where you can decrease or remove any unnecessary challenge. If you don't enjoy mowing your lawn and it brings you down or feels like drudgery, then you can remove that challenge by replacing the lawn with low-maintenance hard landscaping, for example.

By removing simple chores and small stressors that sap your energy and drain your time, you reduce your overall challenge on a regular basis. This frees you up to focus your time and energy on areas that are meaningful for you.

A frequent work challenge for high performers, executives and entrepreneurs is simply having too much to do. The not-enough-time challenge. Additionally, a typical imposter syndrome pattern is a reluctance to ask for help or say no. You might be uncomfortable sharing that your workload is too much because you feel like it's admitting a personal weakness or that you're somehow failing.

Managing the time challenge can be as simple as reviewing priorities. For example, you've got three big projects on and you've been given a fourth. Which one is the most important? Negotiating the deadlines and the priorities can be an easy win if you haven't been doing that already.

You may make promises that you don't have the capacity in your working day to deliver, so work creeps into your personal time. Agreeing timelines or saying yes conditionally, for example 'Yes, I can do that, but not until next week', can help enormously. If you already do this, then this advice is going to sound straightforward, but if it's not something you currently do, it can make a huge difference.

In 2020, Tom Blomfield resigned as CEO of Monzo Bank, citing burnout.[31] In an interview, he revealed that he'd been discussing his overwhelm with the board for a year before his resignation. Although they were concerned, Tom explained, neither he nor the board treated this with enough urgency to take action, such as hiring an interim while searching for the right candidate for a permanent role. At one point, Tom was trying to do the work of four executives while waiting to hire new ones. This is unsustainable, and so it's no wonder that it led to his burnout.

The human and the business cost of burnout is extreme. In 2023, for example, Swiss executive burnout clinics cost $40,000 and had a six-month waiting list.[32]

Therefore, it is essential to address a work culture in which continual overwork is the norm. An overwork culture gives the illusion of being a high-performance culture, but in fact it creates systemic lower performance. This is because a chronically activated nervous system reduces your ability to perform at your best, as we saw in the last chapter on neuroregulation.

When you get the level of challenge right and reduce the unnecessary stressful challenges, then you can stay in the realm of high performance. You get the big, exciting projects and you have the resilience and the capacity to manage the level of stress that a high-performance job requires. Work becomes exciting and it's an adventure that is very satisfying.

Balancing challenge and support

Challenges can also trigger the nervous system due to insufficient support. In fact, the difference between having a positive or a negative challenge is often down to the level of support. When you have enough support, then high challenge can become nothing more than a good stretch.

Social and emotional support is, of course, important and can come from family, friends, peers, mentors, counsellors, coaches, priests etc, but support does not necessarily mean having a 'cheerleader'. Great support is also practical and comes from anything that reduces the overall level of stress in your life.

Although challenge and stress are cumulative, the good news is that support is also cumulative. The more support you get, the less overall stress you experience. This means you're less likely to get triggered and stuck in the cycle of imposter syndrome symptoms. Then, even if your nervous system is triggered, it will be less severe in the presence of good support.

What do I mean by support? At work, it can look like an encouraging boss, a positive environment and getting the training that you need. It can be having effective systems within the company, clear prioritisation of projects, a mentor or a great human resources team.

Support in relationships comes not only from family, but can also be a good friend with whom you can talk things through. They listen without judging you, without trying to fix you or dismiss what you're saying. People tend to keep imposter syndrome a secret, which leads to them feeling isolated and that they don't belong. Having somebody who can listen to and accept you helps reduce that feeling of isolation.

Support in finances can be a professional advisor, a bookkeeper or an accountant. It can also be creating a financial cushion for yourself or finding somebody who could help you out financially just in cases the need arises.

Logistics support is getting help with day-to-day living, for example, household chores, taking the children to school and travelling to work. Anything that you don't enjoy doing or adds to your to-do list is a good candidate for finding extra support. You can even hire people to organise your vacations for you!

Dependents include the elderly, children or anyone else needing specialist care. Here, support can be as simple as getting a tutor for a child or a regular baby-sitter. It can also be accessing community care facilities, daytime activity centres and support groups.

Support around your health can include going to the doctor for a check-up, getting a physical therapist or training coach, or seeing a nutritionist. Support around your hobbies and pastimes can be retreats, training courses, local groups and programmes.

There are one-off events, such as a court case, that happen throughout life and can be highly stressful, so get as much support here as you can. This includes somebody to talk things through with on a personal level, as well as sound professional advice.

Prioritise support. It's not a 'nice to have' and it's not cheerleading. The more quality support you receive, the more resilient you will be and the less imposter syndrome and all its related stress will affect you. The examples I've shared may seem like small things, but when you're operating in a high-challenge environ-ment, every bit of support that reduces your stress can make the difference between the challenge being positive or negative.

Of course, the greater the challenge you take on, the more support you will need to stay on the positive side of the line. When you have the right support to balance the challenge, you'll feel energised and excited in a high-performance role. That is when you are in the best position to achieve your peak potential.

Does imposter syndrome go away by itself?

I often hear people say, 'I had imposter syndrome, but it just went away.' We've seen in this chapter that circumstances trigger imposter syndrome, so it makes sense that when these circumstances improve, the triggers reduce and the imposter syndrome can appear to go away all by itself. However, new triggering circumstances can pop up at any time, and cause the self-doubt and imposter behaviours to come roaring back. In reality, the imposter syndrome has not gone away, it is simply a repeating pattern.

Another situation where imposter syndrome appears to go away all by itself is when people lower their sights and avoid a challenging job or promotion that might trigger it. Avoiding what you know you're capable of reinforces the belief that you are not good enough. It even seems to prove it. Unfortunately, playing it small can lead to deep dissatisfaction and regret. Looking back on your life, you'll know you were capable of so much more and have missed significant opportunities to progress and grow.

Calm triggers

Once you've identified your imposter triggers, managed your time and your stress levels, reduced unnecessary challenges and increased support, your nervous system will get activated less often. As a result, you will feel calmer and lighter on a day-to-day basis.

Taking control of your environment like this reduces the impact of the imposter triggers. However, in life, many things remain outside of your control. These too can trigger imposter syndrome and your nervous system response. Unconsciously, your mind drives you to cope with this physiological stress by trying to do something about it. As a result, you begin imposter behaviours in an automatic attempt to protect yourself from the stress or to try to outperform the situation.

In the next chapter, we'll look at these imposter behaviours, seeing why they're an issue and how you can relax them.

FOUR
Relax Imposter Behaviours

M y first conversations with James explored more of his imposter syndrome symptoms.

'Have you noticed yourself over-preparing for meetings or presentations?' I asked, looking out for classic imposter behaviours.

'All the time,' James replied. 'I know I spend far too much time preparing, but I don't want a question to catch me out, so I cover every possible angle, over and over. It really sucks up my time.'

'Sounds exhausting,' I said. 'How do you get everything done?'

'Ah, I work late, and that often means my two young children are in bed before I get home. I'm not happy about that either, but it seems that's the price of a successful career.'

People with imposter syndrome often struggle to find the right balance between doing enough to do the job well and doing more than is necessary, with diminishing returns on time invested. However, it's not simply the demands of a top job. Typically, the driver is a fear of making mistakes that could potentially expose them as a fraud.

I asked James if he tended to be a perfectionist. He laughed.

'Oh, yes!' he replied. 'I have very high standards, especially for myself. It can sometimes take me an hour just to craft an unimportant email, which is tricky now we have a big project on.'

Most perfectionists are quite open about this behaviour, usually because they see it as the source of their success. They believe they have to be a perfectionist to do their job well, when in actual fact, what they need are high standards. Perfectionism is not high standards, but is intolerance for mistakes. Thus, imperfection becomes a source of distress for them.

'Do you find yourself procrastinating too?' I asked.

'Yes, that one is new, though. My productivity has been dropping recently and that's disturbing. Everything has become harder to do. My work hasn't changed, but it all seems to take more effort these days.'

Procrastinating in imposter syndrome can be an indicator of overwhelm, and it's a warning sign that burnout is a real possibility. You're probably unaware that imposter syndrome is the source of your procrastination. More likely, you are confused by it or frustrated that you procrastinate in the first place.

'I've also noticed that I don't speak up in meetings as much as I want to. It's like I'm less confident to put my ideas forward,' he added.

'Yes, that's the self-doubt showing up as you hiding your opinions,' I replied. 'Although it feels like a sudden lack of confidence, that's not the case. Trying to "talk yourself into having more confidence" won't help here because that's not the problem.'

'Yes, I've tried giving myself a pep talk and it doesn't do much,' reflected James.

Indeed, trying to talk yourself out of imposter syndrome doesn't work. This is because the three symptoms of imposter syndrome – thoughts, physiological stress and behaviours – need to be addressed at the same time.

Imposter behaviours like the ones James described feel a little out of control. They feel automatic or a bad habit you can't seem to shake. This is why many people conclude that there must be something wrong with them. The behaviours increase their sense of self-doubt and reinforce the idea that maybe they're not good enough after all.

Having calmed your physical reactions through neuroregulation and adjusted your environment to reduce stress, you're now ready to tackle the next symptom of imposter syndrome: the automatic behaviours. James described some of the classic imposter behaviour patterns, and you may have several or just one at a time. The exact combination of behaviours is different for everyone, and you have an imposter syndrome profile that is unique to you.

The imposter behaviours are unhelpful, slow you down and hold you back. You may be frustrated by them because you can't seem to get rid of them. It's important to understand that these behaviours are *symptoms* of imposter syndrome and not a character flaw or a weakness.

Imposter behaviours can be further divided into two subcategories: hiding behaviours and striving behaviours. In this chapter, we'll look into each category and what practical steps you can take to relax these behaviours.

Hiding behaviours

These are avoidant behaviours that are an attempt to prevent anyone from 'finding out' that you are not good enough by keeping yourself out of the spotlight.

They include:

- Procrastinating
- Deflecting praise
- Lying
- Hiding your opinions or ideas
- Avoiding promotions or new opportunities

Procrastinating

Procrastination frequently features in imposter behaviours and often goes together with perfectionism and over-preparing. For example, you leave a presentation until the night before it's due, then work late to complete it. Working in this way is stressful and the evening is filled with a fear of failure.

Since you're competent, the presentation will typically go well. When it does go well, however, you don't feel pleased with your work. You suspect that you have fooled everyone yet again or just got lucky, so instead of feeling satisfied by a job well done, you remain anxious and still feel like a fraud. You might also worry that you won't be so lucky or get away with it next time, further increasing your anxiety.

If the presentation goes badly and you are criticised, then counterintuitively, it doesn't feel quite so bad. Of course, you don't enjoy the criticism, but internally you have the excuse that it was a rushed job. It then doesn't feel like a real criticism of your true abilities, and therefore not a real criticism of you as a person. This is the protective driver of procrastination.

Other times, as with James, procrastinating can be due to overwhelm. You have so little energy left that it is a struggle to get things done and all your work takes longer.

Bear in mind that you're unlikely to be aware of the reason for your procrastination. You may just feel confused or frustrated that you procrastinate in the first place.

Deflecting praise

Many people feel uncomfortable being praised, but the imposter experience makes you believe that you don't deserve it. As a result, you want to discount or deflect the praise.

Deflecting praise manifests as apparently polite, modest comments when you're congratulated for a job well done:

- 'I got lucky.'
- 'Anyone could have done it.'

- 'I had plenty of help.'
- 'It was just good timing.'

Such replies are often taken at face value because a truly modest person would make the same polite denials. However, if you were just being modest, these phrases would mean the same to you as polite acceptance of the praise, such as:

- 'Thank you.'
- 'You're very kind.'
- 'Nice of you to say so.'
- 'I'm thrilled it worked out.'

These acknowledge the compliment, but nothing more.

If you feel like a fraud, however, your deflecting phrases are to explain away your success because you genuinely believe that you weren't the cause of it. You minimise your skill, time spent, effort made or the complexity of the task. You worry that you couldn't repeat it and are waiting for the dreaded time when your luck runs out. You may put your success down to outside influences or think that your work is only of value if you do it alone. Any help feels like cheating, which means you don't consider it a personal success.

Deflecting praise is fed by the belief that you have not really earned your success.

Lying

Children are *told* that it's bad to lie, but they discover that they can avoid punishment or disapproval if they do lie. This is how parents unwittingly teach their children to lie.

When you fear people finding out about your mistakes, you may try to hide them and lie to do so. You might dread them being discovered, considering it is proof to others that you are not good enough, so you conceal mistakes rather than bring them out into the open. You may blame others, be evasive or not mention your mistakes at all.

Lying in this defensive manner is an imposter behaviour. It is not a deliberate attempt to deceive, gain something unfairly or to be malicious. It is simply a coping mechanism to protect yourself from disapproval.

Imposter sufferers will try not to make mistakes in the first place. Indeed, the only personality trait researchers could link to imposter syndrome was that sufferers are highly conscientious about their work and hold high standards.[33] When you do eventually make a mistake, however, your fear of being discovered could take over and trigger your nervous system. You know you should be honest, you want to be honest, and yet your fear of being found to be a fraud is greater than your desire to be transparent. Lying is the knee-jerk response to this fear.

If your company culture is one of blame and scape-goating, it further encourages everyone to hide mistakes. The greater the punishment for mistakes, the more you may lie to avoid it.

Hiding the mistake increases your anxiety too. You may lie awake at night, guiltily berating yourself for your error or for not being honest about it. You may also worry that at any moment you could be fired because someone could catch you in the lie.

Hiding opinions

The imposter behaviour of hiding your opinions and ideas looks like not speaking up in discussions, even when you have something useful to say. You might censor yourself for fear of being judged, criticised, mocked or thought to be foolish or stupid.

When you don't share your ideas, you might then get frustrated when someone else says what you wanted to say. You don't get the credit for your ideas and it makes you less visible. Alternatively, you might wait for others to express their opinions before revealing yours, to make sure that at least some people agree with you. You might even say what others want to hear rather than your genuine thoughts on the subject to avoid disapproval or conflict.

Hiding your opinions does not mean that you *never* speak up, nor does it mean that you're shy. Many highly effective executives report that they don't contribute in discussions as much as they would like to, for fear of being found out to be a fraud.[34] The consequences of not speaking up enough are that you're not having the impact that you want to, and your company misses out on your creativity, insights and contribution.

Avoiding opportunities

As we saw earlier, 30% of high achievers report that they don't feel like a fraud, but that doesn't mean that 30% feel good enough about themselves. Many simply avoid the situations that trigger imposter syndrome for them.

You might refuse a promotion or a new job that involves your imposter activity, for example, as you would not want to risk a potential 'failure'. This was my experience with imposter syndrome; I was offered a fast-track leadership position after graduating, but I declined and went back to university to study for a PhD. The risk of failing as a leader was too uncomfortable, even though I didn't recognise it as imposter syndrome at the time.

Avoiding opportunities might entail cancelling interviews using highly creative excuses. As a consultant or business owner, you might not quote for projects, even though you are fully capable of delivering them. Like me, you could be unaware that you are avoiding difficult situations, and it seems like you're simply making 'more interesting' choices.

Throughout her career, fifty-three-year-old pharmaceutical company CEO, Maria, had been slow to step up to her next promotion. Even though her career was successful in many ways, Maria knew she'd gone more slowly than she could have. She estimated she'd delayed each promotion by two years and realised that she could have reached her CEO position twelve years earlier, which would have been an exciting and satisfying career journey for her. She also calculated that she'd effectively missed out on well over $1m in salary over that time through being slow to accept the opportunities offered.

This is not to say that an extremely fast career progression is the only yardstick. Just that Maria realised that she had held herself back from what she was capable of, due to her self-doubt.

Some people stay in one company or even one role for many years, despite feeling uncomfortable or no longer enjoying it. If you believe that you got your job by mistake or through good luck, then you may convince yourself that no one else would hire you if you tried to make a change, and so you stay stuck.

Avoiding opportunities will show up in any area where you feel you're not good enough. People sometimes call this self-sabotage, which is unhelpful because it suggests that this behaviour is a character flaw rather than a symptom of imposter syndrome.

Striving behaviours

Striving imposter behaviours are an attempt to make yourself 'better' somehow. You judge that you are not good enough and think that if you work harder and make no mistakes, then you can rectify this.

The problem with these striving behaviours is that they are exhausting. You work hard for longer than is necessary and worry more and more about your work.

Typical striving behaviours include:

- Perfectionism
- Over-preparing
- Comparing
- Not having enough
- Pushing through

Perfectionism

You may be a perfectionist about your appearance, which is the most recognised form of perfectionism. You are well groomed, immaculately turned out and get upset when your clothes, hair, accessories etc become messy or dirty. You might extend that perfectionism to your possessions, such as your house and car, and to your children and spouse.

Not all perfectionism is visual, however. You may be relaxed about your appearance, but be a perfectionist about being right and knowledgeable. Similarly, you can be a perfectionist about your work performance, fitness, social interactions and more. The key identifier for perfectionism is an intolerance for your mistakes, which distresses you.

Perfectionism is a common imposter behaviour. You may agree logically that absolute perfection is unrealistic and impossible to achieve, but somehow, the impossibility of it doesn't apply to *you*. Internally, you feel that you do need to be perfect.

You might call it 'high standards' and consider it a virtue or even part of your personality, but it's neither. High standards are a great goal to aim for, but perfectionism is the *need* to be flawless and the anxiety and frustration when something falls short of that. In that, you assume that imperfection is proof that you are not good enough. You criticise yourself and fear that others will see your imperfect results and reject you for being a fraud.

Over-preparing

Over-preparing is putting more time and effort into a project than it requires. You might not see it as a problem and just consider yourself to have a good work ethic. Indeed, traditional workplaces often won't see this as a problem either, valuing a thorough job, but over-preparing has a high price. You spend too much time working and it's massively inefficient.

There is a difference between appropriate effort for the task and working yourself into the ground to achieve an unnecessary result. Excessive effort is unsustainable and easily leads to burnout and stress-related illness. It's not a long-term, balanced or healthy strategy.

Being well prepared is, of course, a good practice, as is being thorough, but over-preparing behaviour is quite different. It is driven by anxiety and an overwhelming sense that you *must* excessively prepare to succeed. However, when you over-prepare you likely notice diminishing returns, and the extra time you spend preparing makes less and less difference to the quality of your work. As a result, you experience dread when starting a new project, anticipating how much this is going to cost you in time and effort.

Sometimes people try to control this behaviour by pro-crastinating so that they won't have enough time to over-prepare before a deadline hits. However, this 'solu-tion' is accompanied by all the same worries and stress.

Comparing

We live in a society that constantly compares. We measure, compete and evaluate everything and every-one. Who is faster, stronger, smarter, more attractive, wealthier – you name it, we compare it.

With imposter syndrome, you compare yourself with others, just as most people do. Specifically, you compare other people's apparent success on the outside to the self-doubt and stress that you feel on the inside. However this is not a valid comparison because most people keep their innermost doubts a secret. When you take other people at their surface value, you over-simplify their emotions and assume their inner feelings match their outwardly successful appearance. This is often untrue.

When you compare yourself to your colleagues, it may seem that it's just you who feels like a fraud and you think you don't belong in this job, team, company or at this level. When your colleagues are also high achievers, the differences appear even greater. You find it hard to imagine that these brilliant, confident colleagues feel anywhere near the internal conflict that you do. Of course, you don't see that they may be suffering from imposter syndrome too because people seldom talk about their doubts and self-judgements.

Not having enough

James's wife teased him about having too many letters after his name and his constant urge to get 'just one more' qualification or certification. For James, it always seemed that the next qualification would finally mean he could prove to himself that he was good enough, but it never did.

This less-visible imposter behaviour is feeling like you never have enough. For example, not having enough qualifications, money, experience, companies or material possessions. No matter how much you attain, you have a continued desire for more.

Note that this is not about students getting their career-starting qualifications. Not having enough qualifications refers to the urge to have more when you already have enough for your role and career aspirations. Indeed, I have seen several high performers spend over $200,000 on an executive MBA programme. Although this MBA is a great career asset, these high performers enrolled hoping that it would make them feel less like an imposter and more like they belonged. Needless to say, they were disappointed when, MBA in hand, their feelings about themselves had not changed.

Not having enough applies to money too. Some people unconsciously believe that more money will cure their dissatisfaction with themselves. While money can solve practical problems and make life easier, it doesn't help emotionally. This is why we see a clichéd pattern of a wealthy person working hard to get their next million, ten million, and then billion, but still not being satisfied. This pattern can be labelled as greed, often unfairly as it can easily be the imposter behaviour of accumulation in an attempt to feel better about themselves rather than to revel in material luxury.

With this behaviour pattern, each milestone you hit is never quite enough and you're still emotionally uncomfortable. Your thinking is stuck in the false assumption that the solution must be even more money, qualifications, possessions etc.

Pushing through

The feelings that come up with imposter syndrome are uncomfortable, including self-doubt, self-judgement, not feeling good enough, anxiety and the fear of being found out. You may attempt to escape those feelings by suppressing them entirely, gritting your teeth and pushing through. You hope that if you ignore the discomfort and carry on, then it will eventually go away.

You push through the stress, and focus on working harder for longer than ever before. Work develops a sense of urgency and you approach it tensely, sometimes with a feeling of dread. Challenges become threats to be overcome and not projects that could be fun to test your skills against.

This is especially true if you think that imposter syndrome is the discomfort of still learning or growing in your career. Here, you assume that once you are successful enough, self-doubt and all the other uncomfortable feelings will disappear. Once you are *really* successful, you say, then you will feel better. Unfortunately, because success does not change your feelings about yourself, this moment never comes. You can't out-succeed imposter syndrome.

Being driven to succeed is often seen as a good thing by high achievers, but 'driven' in this context tends to mean driven by fear of failure, criticism, public ridicule or not feeling good enough. Many people are so used to being driven by fear that they mistakenly think it is normal or the only way to succeed. Culturally, men tend to be encouraged to ignore their feelings more, grit their teeth and suffer any pain to get the job done, so they may be more prone to this imposter pattern than women.

These imposter behaviours are not the whole problem, so the solution is not to fix them. It is better to see them as symptoms that you can manage until you are in a position to tackle the underlying cause of imposter syndrome.

Gradual exposure

If you were to try to address all of the imposter behaviours at once, you'd risk overwhelm or triggering your nervous system. It's better to work through them one at a time. The best method I've found so far is called gradual exposure – a process used by therapists to help people with phobias.

For example, say someone comes to a therapist to get rid of arachnophobia, the fear of spiders. The therapist doesn't start by getting them to hold a live spider. That would be too much and would immediately put the patient into the fight, flight or freeze state. Instead, the therapist breaks down exposure to spiders into tiny steps and together, they take one step at a time.

The first step might be talking about insects in general. Once the patient is comfortable and familiar with that discussion, the therapist might talk about the number of legs of different insects. Only when the patient is relaxed in that discussion will they move on to discussing the number of legs on a spider, which is a common trigger for arachnophobes.

The gradual exposure method slowly gets the patient comfortable with each small step, making sure their nervous system doesn't get triggered. This process is also excellent for relaxing the imposter syndrome behaviours.

Neuroscience of gradual exposure

The key to gradual exposure is to get calm and stay calm. This is why we first need to develop our neuroregulation skills and manage our external environment too.

We can't just say, 'Well, that event happened years ago, so it doesn't have any effect on me.' It still does. It has an effect on the unconscious level because the amygdala has retained whatever upset us, frightened

OUTSMART IMPOSTER SYNDROME

us or worried us in the past and is watching out for a repeat performance of that threat.

The gradual exposure technique creates new experiences that feel safe, and so generates memories that don't trigger the amygdala. By having safe experiences as you inch closer to the object of your fear, you decrease the amygdala activity and slowly update what it considers to be a threat. Neuroscientists call this 'fear extinction'. Taking it step-by-step and giving the amygdala a different experience of an old 'threat' eventually reduces its identification of the situation as a life-threatening experience.

Small steps

With imposter syndrome, you can create a small-step gradual exposure plan to help manage the various behaviours. The goal here is not to kick the habit of these behaviours – that would require you to resolve the root cause of imposter syndrome. The goal of gradual exposure is to decrease the stress that the behaviour creates. This breaks the cycle of imposter symptoms and brings a greater level of calm and control.

The small steps you use will depend on which imposter behaviour you're addressing. I recommend you take one behaviour at a time so as to avoid triggering your nervous system, which would defeat the object entirely. In gradual exposure, going slowly is best.

Small gradual exposure steps for **procrastination** would be doing a little bit of whatever project you're delaying. This can be tackling manageable chunks of the project, as in the classic 'How do you eat an elephant? One bite at a time.' Of course, this needs to be done well ahead of the deadline, not in a last-minute rush.

Alternatively, you can work on a small chunk of the project on a time basis rather than on a task basis. For example, spend ten minutes on this project, and then stop and do something else. Adjust the timescale and/or the size of the task until you can comfortably do that one small step in the project.

Once you've done that step, stop, relax and congratulate yourself. When you're calm again, you can do another small piece of work or a short amount of time. Both ways allow you to make steady progress on the project and mean that you can stop judging yourself for having done too little.

If your major behaviour is **deflecting praise**, the first step is to respond by simply saying thank you the next time you are praised. No other response. Just thank you.

After some practice, you can stop deflecting the praise in your head too. In other words, you're saying thank you internally as well as out loud.

Later, you can add more conversational elements, such as saying what you enjoyed about the project, item or event. Saying what you liked about something prompts your brain to look out for things you enjoy in your daily work. In preparing yourself for your next response to praise, you're also connecting with your satisfaction in your work. This is a definite plus!

In the same way, approach **lying** with little gems of honesty that do not trigger you. This behaviour is less responsive to the gradual exposure technique because it is a stronger reaction to the root cause of imposter syndrome, which we'll discuss in the next chapter. However, becoming more aware of the times you defensively lie can be beneficial, so long as you don't criticise yourself for it. Remember, this behaviour is only a symptom of the stress that imposter syndrome is causing you.

Hiding opinions is addressed by speaking up in small ways. Initially, you may need to do this outside of work.

It can help to view this as an experiment. Speak up in a small way about something you would have kept quiet about before, then watch the reactions of those around you. Is it the disaster you were worried about?

This can also be one of the trickier imposter behaviours to shake because it taps deeply into the fear of being found out to be a fraud. You may need to wait until you have changed the underlying cause, which we will cover in Chapters 6 and 7.

Gradual exposure for **avoiding opportunities** would be taking small steps towards what you've been avoiding. However, opportunities like new roles, contracts or promotions don't come around daily.

The small step in this case is to become more aware of your *thinking* behind turning down opportunities. You may notice that you have a gut reaction to the thought of a new opportunity. Try to look at it as a symptom of imposter syndrome and not a personal flaw.

If your imposter behaviour is **perfectionism**, you can start with making a small deliberate mistake. Then sit back and observe what happens.

If that's too much of a leap, rather than making a deliberate spelling mistake on a report that goes to your boss, for example, make it a deliberate mistake outside of work entirely or in a less critical environment until you are comfortable with small mistakes or errors around you.

Once making a small mistake no longer upsets you, move on to the next small mistake. Note that this does not mean that you drop your standards and start doing low-quality work. These small steps are experiments to build your tolerance of mistakes so that the stress of perfectionism does not dominate your work.

Tackling **over-preparing** with gradual exposure can simply be to prepare a little less and observe what happens. Measure the small steps by setting time limits on your preparation too.

One difficulty with over-preparing is that you may not realise what amount of preparation is appropriate and how much is too much. Here, it would be useful to ask for feedback about a suitable level of your preparation from someone you trust.

Comparing has a huge element of self-judgement. You evaluate other people's apparent success on the outside and compare it to the discomfort you feel on the inside. As we've seen before, this is an invalid comparison.

Comparing is a natural part of the brain's survival mechanism: it looks for danger by spotting what has changed. This means that you can't just tell yourself to stop comparing.

Instead of looking for differences and how you might not measure up, focus on the similarities between you and other successful people. See how many similarities you can find. This doesn't stop you from comparing, but it does make you feel closer to others, and helps you feel less isolated and more like you belong.

Not having enough for successful people is often about qualifications or money. Small steps include noticing when you get the urge to take another course, for example. Realise that this urge is a reaction to stress. Spend enough time to get calm once more, and then explore the pros and cons of the course, understanding that it will not get rid of the nagging self-doubt. The more you cultivate this inner calm, the less you'll need to use qualifications as a coping mechanism, and you can choose any new courses or new income ventures from a rational point of view.

The small steps to ease the habit of **pushing through** are taking short breaks and regularly creating time to calm your nervous system. The neuroregulation techniques in Chapter 2 are good for this, especially connecting all your physical senses to your environment.

For all of these imposter behaviours, gradual exposure reduces the stress and the self-judgement that inflames imposter syndrome thinking. It encourages you to become more skilled at observing your nervous system state too.

It is essential to only use gradual exposure when your nervous system is in the calm fellow state. This alone will help to calm your overall levels of stress.

You also don't want to rush gradual exposure techniques. It takes your amygdala and nervous system time to get used to changing its responses to what it once considered a threat. It is best to expose yourself to the fear, and then sit back and process it. You may have to repeat the same experience several times until it feels comfortable and normalised. If you try to rush through the gradual exposure experience too quickly, you are likely to overwhelm your system and it might exacerbate the issue.

High achievers are often keen to go fast, so you may be tempted to do one small step straight after another. At some point, that would trip you into the fight, flight or freeze state, which is just going to reinforce the amygdala's perception of danger. Faster is not better for gradual exposure.

Calm patterns

The last three chapters have demonstrated how and why you can relax your physical body, control your environment and calm down reactive coping behaviours. These steps alone dial down the stress and therefore lessen the impact of imposter syndrome significantly. Treating the symptoms simultaneously breaks the cycle and leads to you feeling calmer, lighter and more in control.

Have you noticed the underlying theme in these last three chapters?

The common theme is neither criticising nor judging yourself for any of the symptoms you experience. This is the secret to calming your physiology, environment and behaviours. All imposter syndrome symptoms are the logical, natural response to a perceived threat and stressor. They are *not* flaws or faults in your personality. You're not broken.

Now that you have calmed the symptoms and disrupted their self-sustaining cycle, you are ready to take the next big step and remove the root cause of imposter syndrome.

FIVE

Freedom Framework

*A*t this stage, James was already feeling so much better. His days were consistently calmer, he was more relaxed, less stressed and sleeping better than he had in a long time. From here, he got curious.

'Why do imposter syndrome symptoms strike even though I know that I'm good at what I do?' he asked. 'Why would I think I'm not good enough when the evidence shows that I am doing well?'

This is the turning point in the process of outsmarting imposter syndrome. Once you have broken the cycle of the symptoms and dialled down the stress, the next step is to tackle to the root cause.

The answer to James's questions lies in the brain's internal model of the world – our beliefs. In this chapter, we look at what beliefs are, how they are formed and what that means for imposter syndrome. We uncover the belief that lies at the heart of imposter syndrome and how it manifests. Then we explore a powerful way to understand others that allows us to release the pain associated with imposter syndrome.

Beliefs

Your brain is a 'prediction machine', according to the latest theories of human consciousness.[35] It is wired to try to predict what will happen in the next few moments so that you are kept safe and that your brain can manage your body's energy reserves efficiently.[36] The more accurate your brain's internal model, the better it can predict the immediate future.

From the very beginning, your brain has been figuring out how your environment works. It creates a vivid internal model of the external world within the quiet darkness of your skull. This internal model includes beliefs about the world. These are your brain's short-cuts to avoid spending unnecessary time and effort analysing a routine situation.

The brain uses 20% of your physical energy, which makes it calorie-intensive and was expensive for our ancestors when their calorie intake was uncertain.[37] Therefore, creating beliefs reduces the amount of energy used by the brain, which is positive for human survival in an uncertain world.

Beliefs allow you to interact quickly and automatically with your environment, so they are a survival mechanism essential for functioning in the world. When you step out on to a road, for example, you are using a belief that the road is solid and can support your weight. You don't waste time tentatively putting out your foot to test the ground with every step.

Such beliefs put everyday interactions on the back burner as far as the brain is concerned, freeing up the thinking mind to pay attention to important new things in the environment, such as potential danger, solving problems creatively and thriving.

Belief is a general term for the brain's shortcuts (psychologists use the word schema too). You hold beliefs about your physical environment, as I just mentioned. You also hold beliefs that are opinions, such as what is a good stock to invest in right now, or which school would suit your child. Some beliefs are affiliations, such as which is the best football team or political party. Other beliefs are what we hold to be true, including religious beliefs and personal values. We also have deeper beliefs about our identity. Finally, there are beliefs about what constitutes a threat to our survival.

We will be focusing exclusively on this last category of belief while discussing imposter syndrome. That is, we will look at what the amygdala determines as a threat, and how our beliefs drive the automatic reaction that we experience.

Developing our beliefs

Our human senses send billions of bits of information to our brains every minute, but a baby's brain is unable to make sense of this. The information is like a huge, undifferentiated mush. As a baby grows, their brain must start identifying distinctions and building its internal model piece by piece.

When we're children, our internal model develops primarily though observation and copying. Sometimes, we're explicitly taught something, such as social behaviour, and we're told, 'This is the way this works.' Other times, the beliefs we pick up are modelled by the people around us or implied by what isn't said or done.

Because we act automatically from our beliefs, we rarely think about them. As children, we don't have an adult's perspective or a sophisticated understanding of the world, so we would not question the beliefs we're adopting or even realise they could be questioned. However, we also rarely choose these beliefs deliberately. Therefore, it's no surprise that as adults, we generally never question our belief systems either.

If nobody in our family had learned a particular skill, it's far less likely that we would have developed that skill without focused effort ourselves.

For example:

- Pick a language that you don't know – say, Japanese.

- If you don't speak Japanese, why not?

- Because you were never taught Japanese.

- Why didn't your parents teach you Japanese?

- Because they didn't know Japanese, so naturally they couldn't teach it to you.

- Why didn't they know Japanese?

- Because nobody had taught them.

This pattern repeats for all kinds of skills, including navigating relationships, dealing with difficult situations and in leadership roles.

When we attribute our lack of skill, knowledge or a particular belief to our parents and the environment that we grew up in, this is not to blame our parents. This is not being disloyal, judging or criticising parents for what they teach children. The people teaching us were doing the best they could with the knowledge, beliefs and resources that they had.

Other life skills include how we manage our own frustration and anger. If our parents didn't learn how to manage their anger well, there's a good chance we won't know how to deal with our own anger either. Again, there's no blame here. It's just what was demonstrated to us as behaviour options when we were children.

Some beliefs we're aware of, but most are completely unconscious. While some beliefs are positive, accurate and helpful, others are not. One belief in particular is the root cause of imposter syndrome.

The happy belief

In the 1950s, one of the grandfathers of personal psychology, Dr Carl Rogers, embarked on a great quest.[38] He wanted to discover the source of happiness, specifically what makes a person happy, regardless of what difficulties life throws at them.

He reviewed his experience with thousands of clients, and he found the answer he was looking for! He concluded that real and lasting happiness, freedom from suffering, is caused by a belief in our inherent and unconditional self-worth, instilled from a rare and remarkable childhood.

Unfortunately, he also discovered that the vast majority of us (99.95%)[39] believe the opposite, that our worth depends on what we do. That is, our worth is conditional.

Conditional worth says, 'If I *do* something good, I *am* good. If I *do* something bad, I *am* bad.' It confuses a moral judgement of our actions with a judgement of our innate worth. The belief in our conditional worth is usually unconscious, and so few people express it in this way. It is also a belief that runs through all societies and cultures in the world, so most people don't even notice this belief, nor the negative effect it has on them.

The problem with conditional worth is that it leaves our mood, emotions and sense of self entirely at the mercy of life's circumstances. It then becomes all too easy to dislike, disapprove of or even hate ourselves.

Rogers discovered that the false belief of conditional worth was established in early childhood, but he was deeply disappointed because he knew no way to change that belief in adults. At that time, neuroscience (the study of the brain) was in its infancy. The brain's internal model was thought to become fixed and unchangeable by adulthood. However, in the 1980s, neuroscientists started to agree that the brain is not fixed after all.[40] It has neuroplasticity, which is the ability to change and even grow new brain cells, but by this time, the world had moved on and forgotten about Rogers' ground-breaking discovery.

Except, that is, for a few isolated Worth Coaches and therapists who had discovered ways to shift the worth belief from conditional to unconditional.

Unconditional worth

The key to happiness, said Rogers, is having a sense of our unconditional worth. That is, what we do, good or bad, has no influence on who we are.

This is a radical idea for many people. Here's one way to think about it. Consider the time of your birth. Newly born, you were completely worthwhile, an absolute miracle and a delight. You hadn't done anything to earn that: no words, no actions and no favours. You were just there and 100% worthy of being loved and cared for.

The insight of unconditional worth is that this fact has never changed from the moment you were born until right now. You are still completely worthy, completely lovable, completely adorable and a miracle. Nothing has changed between then and now. When you believe your worth is unconditional, it frees you to explore your limits of achievement without fear of being bad, wrong, rejected or unloved.

Learning our worth

Rogers found that whether we develop conditional or unconditional worth depends on how we were brought up as a child. Therefore, conditional worth starts in early childhood.

Before children develop a sense of self (an 'I') at between eighteen months and three years old, they do not perceive boundaries between themselves, their experiences and the world around them.[41] When a small child is told that something they have done is wrong, it is identical – in their perception – to being told that *they* are wrong. Bad. Disapproved of. This is the perfect time in childhood development to be taught that worth is unconditional.

However, if a child is not taught that their worth and actions are separate, then the conclusion their mind makes is: 'When I make a mistake, my parents are disappointed or annoyed. When I do something wrong, I get told off. Therefore, I must be bad. There must be something wrong with me. I'm not good enough.'

We learned this from the different reactions of our parents and guardians according to what we did. If we were good, tidy and polite, then we likely got smiles and approval. If we were successful and did well at school, we likely received smiles and approval. Now, some people's childhoods were not filled with smiles or approval; they just got less disapproval for being tidy, clever or polite etc. Some people even had cruel or abusive childhoods where approval was minimal or non-existent.

You might assume that the degree of approval or disapproval makes a difference to whether we develop conditional worth, but it doesn't.[42] The degree of the response is less important than the fact that there was any difference at all between the reactions when we behaved well versus those when we made mistakes. Even a twitch of an eyebrow or a hint of a frown can convey disapproval, and at that moment we feel unacceptable, reinforcing the belief that our worth is conditional.

Regardless of which childhood experiences you had, they taught the same belief of your worth being conditional. You learned that it is not enough to be who you are. Conditional worth became part of your identity, so as an adult you, and almost everyone else, believe that your worth depends on what you do.

Why is this one belief so powerful? Why is it the root cause of whether we're happy and satisfied in our lives or not? The explanation comes from simple biological survival.

When a baby is born and for many years during their childhood, they are completely dependent on their parents and guardians to be looked after. If a child is not cared for, fed, clothed, kept warm and held, they will die.[43] Biologically, we must be cared for as infants. Implicitly, we must be found *worth* caring for by our caregivers.

This creates a potential danger situation in young brains: 'If I'm not worth this care and attention, then I will die.' It is wholly unconscious. It's unlikely that we'd ever say to ourselves, 'If my parents don't approve of me, I'll die', but survival fear creates this perception.

If we feel unworthy in this way, then it creates strong feelings of emptiness, being alone and unlovable, coupled with a fear of dying. Unlovable: if we're not loved, if we're not cared for, we will die. Alone: if we're left alone, if we're abandoned, we will die.

The brain treats emotional pain and physical pain as the same,[44] and so the strong emotional pain of conditional worth spurs the brain into trying to do anything to avoid it in order to survive.

Survival strategies

The huge feelings of being empty, helpless, alone and unlovable are so overwhelming for children that they naturally find a way to escape them by developing 'survival strategies'. Almost everyone developed these survival strategies. The question is not whether we developed them or not, but which ones we developed.

There are five major survival strategies.[45] As children, we tried these out, homing in on one or two as most effective for surviving our individual circumstances. These are:

- Power
- Approval or praise
- Distraction
- Safety
- Drama

Power

We use the survival strategy of power to feel more in control of ourselves and/or other people. This might mean we are bossy or authoritarian. We might feel superior or act like we are. In the extreme, power might manifest as bullying.

The driver behind reaching for power is to feel strong rather than helpless or weak. You feel more comfortable when you are in charge and in control of yourself, other people and the events around you.

Approval or praise

If your major survival strategy is to get approval and praise, you will always be working to do the right thing. You may tend to want to be right and you might have tried to be a perfect boy or girl growing up.

This is the 'golden child' who's successful and works hard not to be disapproved of. Sometimes, they turn to people pleasing to get approval. When they get the approval from praise, then in that moment they might feel that they are worthwhile.

The problem with praise is that it must be continually earned, which can be exhausting. However, the bigger problem is that your feelings of worth are heavily based on the opinions of others and therefore out of your control.

Distraction

The survival strategy of distraction is used to try and escape from our current reality. Escaping from the terrible feelings of unworthiness, numbing ourselves so that we don't feel the pain of it.

The numbing can be chemical, like using alcohol, cigarettes or drugs, both recreational or prescription. It can be emotional eating or excessive exercise, the high of gambling, a sex or shopping addiction, or doing extreme sports. More recently, we've seen addictive video games, compulsive social media scrolling, online porn and binge-watching a box set, all to numb the strong feelings.

The driver behind this survival strategy is to escape from feeling empty, afraid, alone and unworthy.

Safety

The survival strategy of safety is controlling the environment around you so that there are no surprises. This makes you feel less vulnerable to changing situations.

You might develop a rigid routine and get upset or frustrated if that gets disrupted. You might resist change, be risk averse or try to control the environment and the people around you. Unlike the power survival strategy, in which people use control to feel stronger, the safety survival strategy uses control to reduce surprises and increase the perception of safety.

The driver is, 'If I'm more in control of my environment, if I can keep a lock on it, I'm less likely to be harmed. Then, I'm safe.'

Drama

The drama survival strategy is chaos as opposed to rigid routine. It is a loud, high-energy prima-donna approach to the world. It's making a scene and exaggerating emotions. Things are 'massively amazing' or 'absolutely terrible'. It's wanting people to pay attention to you, notice you and sometimes to save you in desperate situations.

The driver behind this strategy is, 'If you pay attention to me, then I can trust I'll be cared for and worthwhile.' Drama draws attention.

For children, being ignored can be more painful than being punished, and negative attention feels preferable to no attention. Drama again taps into the primal fear of abandonment, which to a baby could result in death.

The addictive aspect

All of these survival strategies have a slight 'addictive' element to them, just like drugs are addictive. You get a hit when you first take a drug. Later, the same amount doesn't give you the same response, so you need more. This also happens with survival strategies.

With power, there's a sense of strength and control when you get a promotion at work, for example, but as you get used to that role, you stop feeling the little rush of power as it becomes normal for you. The feeling of strength you were getting from your new position fades, and you want more. This is how people can crave more and more power.

People who use the approval and praise survival strategy struggle because everybody gets used to their level of performance. Over time, they get less praise for the same high performance. Then they feel they have to do even better and work harder to earn more praise, which is unending and exhausting.

It's the same addictive pattern for distraction, safety and drama. The urge is always to get more to continually protect ourselves from the painful feelings of conditional worth.

We can also jump between different strategies depending on the situation. In some circumstances, power simply doesn't work, so we might then go to a secondary strategy and seek praise, for example, or distract ourselves.

Most of us don't realise these survival strategies are related to the painful feelings of conditional worth. In fact, these behaviour patterns appear to be a part of our personality, which is incorrect. We developed them as children to deal with difficult feelings and to avoid the emotional pain associated with them. It was our best way of coping.

It's crucial to understand that these strategies are used by almost everybody when under stress. The more pressure a person is under, the more activated their nervous system, the more they will turn to their survival strategies. Since most people are unaware of their survival strategies, this part of their behaviour is also unconscious.

This knowledge is a powerful framework for understanding yourself and other people. When used to develop empathy for human behaviour, it becomes the launch pad for accepting yourself and other people, and for developing a rock-solid sense of your own unconditional worth.

Behaviour does not stop at survival strategies, so let's go deeper and look at additional patterns.

Compensating behaviours

Sometimes, we don't get the response from others that our survival strategy demands, or the situation doesn't allow it. When that happens, we switch to compensating behaviours to try to get back to the 'better' feeling we seek from our survival strategy.

For example, if we're not getting the approval that we normally get, then we might use compensating behaviour to persuade other people to give us that approval. Again, this is not a deliberate act, but an unconscious pattern, driven by the need to avoid the pain of conditional worth.

There are five major compensating behaviours, either to get something from somebody else or to protect ourselves from a situation. This comes from the work of Dr Greg Baer, who's been helping adults break free from conditional worth for over thirty years.[46] He identified these five different behaviours that people exhibit when they don't get their 'drug of choice' from their survival strategy:

- Attacking
- Acting like a victim
- Lying
- Running
- Clinging

Attacking

This is exactly what it sounds like. You might think of it as a physical attack, and certainly, any violence or even intimidation would be just that, but it can also be verbal attacks, anger, slander, sarcasm, sabotage or gossip.

Acting like a victim

Acting like a victim is not the same as *being* a victim. For example, if we're dancing and you step on my foot, then at that moment, I am a victim. I have a painful foot because you've stepped on it. However, if I then complain to everybody in the room and tell them what a horrible person and a terrible dancer you are, that's *acting* like a victim.

Acting like a victim includes complaining, the sympathy stories that we tell over and over again, blaming other people and putting a 'poor me' spin on a particular situation. The idea behind it is to make us the innocent victim and in the right, with the other person or situation made out to be wrong, bad or a cruel and terrible monster.

Lying

Lying, of course, is simply saying what's not true. It is also misdirection, evasiveness and omission. It is done to avoid attack or punishment, or to manipulate others to get what we want.

Running

Running is sometimes physically leaving the situation, such as walking out of the room. It can even be leaving a job or a relationship.

Running can be withdrawal, maybe refusing to have a conversation with somebody. It can also be emotional withdrawal, ignoring the other person or being distant with them.

Clinging

When we think of clinging, we may think of a child holding onto their mother's leg, not wanting to be left alone or abandoned. As adults, clinging can be pleading, whining and complaining to make the other person feel guilty for not giving us what we want. Being demanding and manipulating like this is an attempt to prevent ourselves from being abandoned.

People use any or all of these compensating behaviours when their survival strategies aren't working or have become less effective. The illustration shows the whole model put together, starting with the root cause, conditional worth, which creates the internal unconscious discomfort.

Conditional worth

⇩

Praise	Power	Distraction	Safety	Drama

⇩

Attack	Act like a victim	Lie	Run	Cling

Neither survival strategies nor compensating behaviours are a deliberate choice, but are instead an automatic reaction to a perceived pain or threat.

People doing their best

This pattern of survival strategies and compensating behaviours represents people doing their very best not to feel worthless and terrible about themselves. They're used when someone feels stressed and their nervous system is activated. When you're aware of these patterns, you will observe them in other people as well as yourself.

Which survival strategy you use depends on what worked when you were growing up. If you're a parent, you'll know that your children are always testing your boundaries. They experiment to find what works best for them.

There's no judgement here. These behaviours don't make you a bad person. Everyone uses them, so there's no need to judge when you see them in yourself. Remember, this is the best option you could find from the tools you learned from your childhood.

When you see survival strategies and compensating behaviours in other people, again, there's no need to judge. This is them doing the best that they can to feel better about themselves, feel more comfortable and to reduce emotional pain.

Freedom

If the only thing you take from this book is an under-standing of survival strategies and compensating behaviours, and use it to look at people differently, then it will create a radical change in your life. You will immediately start seeing people's negative actions and emotional reactivity as a result of unconscious internal pain. It is not their personality, they're simply using these patterns. You will know that their style of communication is the best they've learned. They sim-ply don't have better resources and skills available to them in the moment when their nervous system is activated and their brain is screaming that they're in danger of succumbing to a tsunami of painful feelings.

In that moment, they don't see any other options. Later, on reflection, they might see what they could have done differently, but while their amygdala is in alert mode, they simply can't.

Other people's survival strategies are not about you, they are just an expression of their pain and discomfort filtered through their beliefs about what is possible for them to do next. This knowledge allows you to step out of victimhood and see others as humans, just like you, who are doing the best they can with the resources they have. If you had lived their exact life, with all their experiences, with the same beliefs learned and taught, then you would do the same thing they did. When you see the tragedy of being ruled by the belief that worth is conditional, your compassion naturally bubbles up.

Let's go back to CEO Kim, who we met in Chapter 2, whose typical stress response was the fight state. When she learned about this framework for understanding people's behaviour, she felt like her whole world shifted and settled. She now understood why others behaved as they did. That other people's survival strategies and compensating behaviours, which had instantly triggered her into defensiveness and aggression, were not about her. Breathing a sigh of relief, she saw that their behaviours were not a threat, but rather an expression of pain.

This thinking immediately tempered her response. She now knew the way others behaved towards her was not personal, and so her own system was far less easily triggered. This resulted in her meetings becoming calmer, less confrontational and more productive than ever before.

She also applied the insight to herself and recognised that her own anger and defensiveness were an expression of an activated nervous system. This opened the door for her feeling compassion and acceptance of herself.

The imposter belief

Although almost everyone operates from the unconscious belief of conditional worth, not everyone experiences imposter syndrome. For most highly successful people, conditional worth manifests in their lives as imposter syndrome.

The connection between conditional worth and imposter syndrome is clear. Imposter syndrome has at its core the belief that *I'm not good enough, and if I'm not good enough, then ultimately, it will affect my survival.*

The amygdala will trigger the nervous system to react whenever you feel not good enough. This creates feelings of anxiety, confusion, isolation and overwhelm, which is exactly the experience of believing your worth is conditional. That is, conditional worth is the root cause of imposter syndrome.

Knowing this, you can now appreciate why imposter syndrome affects so many people. It is also clear that it is not an aspect of your personality, culture or gender.

The good news is that there are ways to develop a sense of your unconditional worth as an adult. You're not doomed to a life of misery if you didn't happen to win the childhood 'lottery' that would create unconditional worth.

When the conditional worth belief is in the driving seat, life is a rollercoaster of ups and downs, of reacting to the situation we find ourselves in. How we feel about ourselves is outside of our control, like a leaf blown around in the wind. Our view of ourselves is not stable, which leaves us feeling vulnerable to circumstances.

The conditional worth belief leads to knee-jerk reactivity to difficult situations and using survival strategies and compensating behaviours. These automatic behaviours that are at best unhelpful, and at worst destructive.

What we want instead is to be flexible and responsive to the environment around us. We want to have confidence and a sense of comfort in our own self and worth. We want to be calm, not reactive. Ultimately, we want to be self-aware and choose the things that are supportive and helpful to us.

Most people have no idea that they even have that choice. Eliminating imposter syndrome for good means changing this deep underlying belief from conditional worth to unconditional worth.

In this chapter, we've laid a powerful foundation for upgrading our emotional intelligence. With this framework, we understand people and what drives them without making anyone a monster or a victim. It is possible to use this knowledge to change the way that our amygdala perceives threats in the first place. Then our response becomes automatic understanding and acceptance of others and ourselves. This perspective forms the foundation for using a powerful tool that allows us to finally develop a strong sense of our unconditional worth.

Let's delve more deeply into that next.

SIX
Free Your Mind

Developing unconditional worth is the ultimate way to eliminate imposter syndrome for good. To develop unconditional worth, we first need a consistent way to change the amygdala's perception of a threat. In Chapter 7, we'll then explore the neurochemical mechanism at work and reveal a system that uses this new process to get the belief-change results we want.

We start by understanding how the amygdala creates and reinforces beliefs. We'll look at the amygdala change process itself and the psychology behind it.

Just thinking positively doesn't change triggering beliefs. Standing in front of the mirror and telling yourself you are amazing, confident and good enough rarely works, or if it does help, the feeling rarely lasts.

Why? Because the thinking part of your brain is trying to affirm something that your amygdala and the feeling part of the brain simply doesn't believe. Since the amygdala's purpose is to make sure you survive dangers, then the existing internal model trumps the new self-talk, and you will soon revert back to self-doubt and imposter syndrome.

We have seen in the last four chapters that the amygdala triggers the nervous system response. That is, our beliefs related to our survival are mediated by the amygdala. In fact, the beliefs related to our survival are *stored* in the amygdala.[47]

Therefore, changing a belief must include a permanent way to alter the amygdala's threat assessment. We first need to understand how the amygdala determines what constitutes a threat.

Amygdala key

Some dangers are pre-programmed into the amygdala in our brain from birth, although there are surprisingly few of these. They include deep growls from a predator, heights and snakes. Other hazards are learned during childhood, such as fire, knives and speeding cars. These are all physical threats that could kill or maim us.

Children further discover what is a threat in their environment in many ways, including:

- Dangers taught directly, for example, 'Be careful, that fire is hot. If you touch it, it will burn you.'

- Those taught indirectly, such as comments they overhear, from TV, movies, social media and books, or what's said and demonstrated by people around them.

- Other dangers they conclude from their personal experience or from witnessing someone else's personal experience.

We can learn from any of the above, most of which we don't consciously remember. The amygdala also notes 'threats' that are social, behavioural and emotional, and treats them as if they were life-and-death situations too. For example, it takes the threat of isolation from a group seriously, which is why rejection and abandonment are primal fears buried deep within our psyche.

The self-taught amygdala

In addition to innate and learned threats, your amygdala also creates its own list of dangers without any input from you. It constantly searches for new threats to add to its checklist of dangers.

How does the amygdala decide which situations are dangerous? The answer lies in emotions.

When the brain perceives a threat, the amygdala stores a combination of the information from the senses and the emotion you felt at the time. That is, the brain creates a specific belief about that threat. Neuroscientists call these fear memories, but I refer to them here as *emotion-memories* to emphasise the interconnectedness of emotion and memory.

A strong negative emotion, such as fear, signals to the amygdala that there is something dangerous in your environment. The amygdala cannot tell whether an emotional response is due to physical danger or social discomfort, such as feeling embarrassed, so it treats both as equally threatening. Both scenarios make the danger list that the amygdala continually scans, alert to any hint you might need to take life-saving action.

Emotion-memories

When we have a strong negative emotional reaction to an event, the amygdala effectively 'tags' the sensory information coming into the brain as a possible indication of danger. In doing so, it takes note of all the senses: the sounds, the images, the taste, the smell and the touch. It flags these elements as indicators of potential threats without our conscious involvement.

We see this in the extreme with PTSD where, for example, soldiers have experienced life-threatening dangers. When they return home, they might react to sounds that are normal for their home environment, but the amygdala has labelled those sounds as life-threatening. Thus, a classic PTSD response to a car backfiring is the ex-soldier diving under the table because it sounds like an exploding bomb. Not because the ex-soldier thought about it logically, but because the amygdala responded to the loud noise before any thinking could even occur.

With the amygdala, anything similar to its list of dangers gets added too. In this way, your body can be automatically tripped into a fight, flight or freeze state by situations that are similar to uncomfortable past experiences. You can be triggered, but have no idea why.

Do you have any say?

Everything on the amygdala's list of dangers will 'hijack' your brain and flip you into fight/flight/ freeze states before you can decide logically what's really a threat or not. This might sound like your amygdala causes you to freak out whenever the tiniest of events happens, but there are levels of amygdala activation. You may have a mild flight reaction that you take a breath and can then ignore, or you might have a full-blown 'run screaming from the room' feeling.

It all depends on the level of threat that the amygdala determines and how active it is.

121

Changing emotion-memories

Consider what would happen if you consciously revised the emotion-memories that constitute your amygdala's danger list and switched off the automatic reactivity to things that aren't a genuine threat. In your day-to-day life, you would become less reactive and more patient. Less distracted and more present. Less stressed and more energised. Less defensive and more authentic. Less self-critical and more resilient.

Changing such an emotion-memory must include changing the amygdala's labelling of the situation as a threat. The technique presented here permanently re-patterns the amygdala by using the same biological process that it used to 'learn' this threat in the first place, as we'll see in Chapter 7.

This is a *letting-go* process that systematically defuses the emotional charge of an old emotion-memory. The amygdala is keyed to spot memories with a high emotional charge. However, after letting go it stops seeing that event and those like it as a threat. Practically, this means that the situations that once triggered your nervous system no longer do so.

Freedom from our past

When our thoughts are distracted by negative events from the past, such as failures or painful, uncomfortable situations, it has an impact on our present-day energy, resilience and mood. This in turn has mental effects and impacts our productivity, focus, creativity, problem-solving ability and decision making.

Curiously, the brain does not distinguish between memories and the present moment.[48] When we remember a painful or hurtful thing from the past, the brain treats it as if it's happening right now, as if it's real, and this provokes the unconscious reactivity in us.

Whether the event is large or small, if it triggers the fight, flight or freeze response, then the body reacts as if it is in life-threatening danger. This affects us physically, and when the body continually reacts to past events, it turns into chronic stress.

The letting-go process releases the emotional charge (pain) that the event created in the past so that we don't replay it in the present day. The process is pretty straightforward, even though the neuroscience behind it is complex.

To let go, we move through a carefully choreographed dance, deliberately shifting emotions from neutral to negative, and then up to positive. It is not a purely intellectual process because we are using emotions to facilitate the amygdala change. While it is possible to learn this process alone, it is far easier and more effective when you have someone to guide you through it.

Letting go needs to be done in a specific order to be effective and update the emotion-memory, but once we've done that, the emotional pain of the event is gone. The event becomes a fact we can recall logically, but it doesn't disturb us emotionally any more.

James was unsure of this step, so I walked him though the letting-go process. It took us just twenty minutes on a Zoom call. He started with a tricky situation that had bothered him for years.

Once we were done, James had a strange look on his face: a combination of surprise, delight and a little confusion.

'That's so weird,' he said, laughing. 'It's gone. Well, I can remember the facts, but it's not a sharp dagger in my stomach any more. The edges are soft,' and his hands made the shape of a small, round, decidedly un-daggerlike object. 'It seems more like an old faded photo than a real memory.'

He laughed again. 'It can't be that simple. Let's do another.' We did and he had a similar experience.

James was confused by the speed and efficacy of the letting-go process. It worked so quickly that it seemed unbelievable, even magical, but every step of this carefully crafted process has solid scientific research and decades of experience behind it. Its strength is in its elegant simplicity.

Let's explore the letting-go process that James was so impressed by.

There are eight steps in this belief-clearing letting-go process:

1. Choose

2. Decide

3. Imagine

4. Access

5. Find

6. Understand

7. Feel

8. Celebrate

We'll go into detail for each of these steps, explaining the psychology behind them.

1: Choose

You have past events in your life that were painful, uncomfortable and created negative feelings. They were not life-threatening, but they still cause you an emotional reaction when you remember them. You may experience a quick flash of feeling uncomfortable emotions such as anger, hurt, embarrassment, guilt or outrage, and your nervous system reacts. You could call these events difficult moments or small traumas.

For the first step of the letting-go process, select one such event and one person involved. This targets a specific emotion-memory, that is, one point in time and related to one person. Recalling this accesses the emotion-memory.

If you were to try to do the letting-go process for many events at once, even if they involved the same person and/or similar behaviour, then it wouldn't have the intended clearing effect. Instead, you'd be thinking in terms of a generalised concept stored in a different part of the brain, and it wouldn't alter the emotion-memory.

It is essential to start with small events and not jump into the biggest, most difficult memories. The process requires that you stay in the untriggered fellow state throughout. Too big, and the significant past event would trigger your nervous system, which would prevent the positive change from occurring.

2: Decide

Next, deliberately decide to change the belief or judgement about the situation you want to let go of. It's important to be motivated and determined to make this change. The brain has a normal biological resistance to changing its internal model. After all, this internal model has kept you alive so far. You therefore need deliberate effort to change this kind of belief.

The F-word

You could describe letting go as *forgiving* the other person for their actions in this situation. People often treat forgiveness as a bad word. It can feel counter-intuitive to forgive someone for the hurt they caused you, as if forgiving then means that you are invalidating your pain. Consequently, people often resist forgiving due to what they *think* it means.

You might think that forgiveness means:

- The event wasn't important or significant
- The event wasn't painful
- You have to agree with somebody who did something destructive
- You have to condone the other person's actions
- You have lost somehow
- You would allow it to happen again
- You would become a doormat
- You would have to reconcile, apologise or interact with that person again

None of these is true.

This letting-go process is private, internal and solely for your benefit. It is to release your brain from the emotion-memories that continue to haunt you and that your amygdala uses to flag potential danger.

When you let go of these past events, you will naturally spend more time in the resourceful, calm fellow state. You respond rather than react to what's going on in the moment. It improves your relationships, decision making, problem solving, creativity, focus and productivity. Ultimately, you develop freedom from the past and conscious enjoyment of the present moment, including the people and situations around you.

You are deliberately creating a happier future when you can let go.

Simon was a successful executive, but he and his wife split up after she had an affair. They were going through a bitter divorce and Simon was angry, frustrated and hurt.

The divorce was distracting him at work and impacting how he related to other women, one of whom might potentially become a new partner. He found that he no longer trusted women in personal relationships and was worried that he might have to spend the rest of his life alone and lonely as a result.

When I taught him letting go, he went through it three days in a row, specifically working on letting go of his feelings towards his ex-wife and forgiving her. This changed his attitude towards her dramatically. He found that he understood her and her survival strategies of drama and approval. He could accept her and be kind and generous towards her.

That didn't mean he was going to become a doormat. He understood and accepted her, and he was still going to continue with the divorce proceedings. Just because he'd let go of his negative feelings and forgiven her didn't mean that he wouldn't carry on with the court case and make sure that their joint assets were divided equitably. However, it did mean that he started feeling optimistic that he could have a positive relationship with a new partner in the future.

It's vital to see that in letting go, although Simon forgave his wife, it wasn't for her benefit or even about her. It wasn't letting her get away with anything, nor was it agreeing that her actions were right or justified. The letting go was for *Simon*, for him to clear the negative emotion-memories that were distracting him and causing him not to be present in his life. He gained freedom from this distraction, and from the stress of bitterness and thoughts of the past.

The benefit when you *decide* to let go is that *you* will feel much better.

3: Imagine

Next, imagine the person involved in this event standing in front of you. They're the one you're going to forgive so that you can let go of this emotion-memory.

Like a courtroom official, you calmly charge them with the facts of what they've done. You state the facts only about their words or actions.

They don't get to talk back, argue or defend themselves in your imagination. This is not a dialogue. Instead of judging and punishing them, you will be letting go for your benefit, not theirs. The charge brings the facts of the person and the event to the forefront of your conscious mind, allowing you to start to change this emotion-memory.

4: Access

Now recall your emotional reaction to the event you chose in Step 1. Remember how you felt when the event occurred, not just mentally, but *feeling* it again, reliving the emotion. You might have felt pain, anger, fear, overwhelm, irritation, shame, guilt or anxiety.

If it is a particularly powerful emotion that could potentially overwhelm you, don't dive into it. Instead, just tap into the feeling a little. Conversely, if you know that you tend to avoid or suppress feelings, then make an effort to identify and feel those emotions again more deeply.

If, at any point, these feelings start to become at all overwhelming, then this situation has too high an emotional charge for you to deal with right now. Stop, relax and try later with a less highly charged event.

When you re-experience the complete emotion-memory, it will bring up all your thoughts about it. Typically, these are negative thoughts such as judgement, criticism or blame.

5: Find

Now imagine yourself as an observer, standing off to one side of the event and look for a more positive viewpoint. Mild detachment like this is positive and allows the emotions to become less raw and intense. It dials down the immediacy of the emotion-memory so that you become calmer and less stressed by it.

When the amygdala tags an emotion-memory as dangerous, we tend to view the entire event as negative. It is important to see the event neutrally and this means finding a positive in it.

To find a positive in the event, you step back and become a witness to the bigger picture. You look at what happened around the event itself rather than just the spot of negativity you recall. Find something positive that came out of this event. In psychology terms, this is called reframing.[49]

Saskia's colleague criticised her presentation, implying that she wasn't very good. This motivated her to improve her skills and take a public speaking course. On this course, she met a person who became a wonderful friend.

The negative event was the criticism and the positive outcome was that she made a dear friend. Making a new friend is unrelated to the criticism and Saskia's reaction to it, but it is still something positive that came out of that colleague's original comment.

This doesn't mean that the colleague was right or that Saskia agreed with them. She could just see that there was something positive that arose from their action. A gift or lesson for her came out of it.

The gift or lesson can be just a small positive. It is not intended to make up for the negative or to justify that the event was OK. You're not trying to balance the negativity of the event with the positivity that came out of it.

The gift can come at a different time from the event itself. It might be years later when you look back and realise the lesson that could be learned from that experience. For example, imagine your family moved for work when you were a child. You hated the move and losing all your friends, but it meant you went to a much better school that you loved and it had a positive impact on your education. You can see that as a positive.

If, at this stage, you find it impossible to think of a gift or a positive lesson, then the event you've chosen is probably too big for you to let go of right now. Stop, take a break, and later choose a different, less painful event. Struggling to find a gift may also indicate that you need someone to help you learn how to reframe the event.

This reframing takes you out of the victim mentality. There is a big difference between being a genuine victim in an event and acting like a victim. Being a victim in the moment is experiencing pain and suffering. For all the world, we wish that such things didn't happen, but unfortunately, they do. Acting like a victim or victimhood, on the other hand, is holding on to that feeling of hurt and suffering long after the event.

Victimhood is black and white, having a perpetrator and a victim.[50] It is a rigid view that gives you a feeling of being right and often righteous, and it brings a little sense of power. This rigidity is seductive because being right makes you feel less helpless.

However, being right doesn't help you move on and let the situation go. In fact, victimhood ensures that you remain hurt and haunted by this situation years later so that you can continue to be right about it.

Because of this, victimhood is toxic thinking that hurts only you. It is essential to step out of the victim mentality because it hangs on to the hurt in an attempt to punish the other person or to feel justified in hurting them back. Holding onto victimhood doesn't change what happened, and doesn't hold the other person accountable. It does not achieve anything useful. It is like drinking poison and hoping the other person dies from it, as the saying goes. That is, it only hurts you and your mental, emotional and physical wellbeing.

Seeing yourself as a victim is also disempowering. It reinforces the idea that you are helpless, powerless and unsafe, which impacts how you see yourself and your own worth and how you interact with the world.

When you reframe the event to find a positive, you start to release the solid grip of victimhood because you can see that you have benefited in some way. At this point, focus on feeling pleased about or grateful for this gift.

6: Understand

Now that your brain is primed to change, you create a second reframe about why the other person did what they did. Rather than ascribing it to their personality or labelling them a bad person, instead, consider their actions to be a logical response based upon their knowledge, beliefs and skills, as we saw in Chapter 5.

Consider their survival strategies

Understand the other person as much as you can. This is the intellectual part of this reframing process. Your thoughts here help to change the way that you feel about the incident through the deliberate process of reframing the other person's actions and assumed motivations.

Consider which habitual survival strategies and/or compensating behaviours that person used. Look at what was happening in the rest of their life and any stressors there. Think about what resources they had then, including information, financial, mental, emotional and physical resources. Which skills did they have or lack? Which beliefs did they hold? See the event from their point of view.

Realise that their words and actions were a result of their habitual survival strategies, done so as not to feel worthless. Yes, their behaviour was clumsy, inelegant and maybe even ugly, but unconsciously, they were trying to feel better about themselves. Unfortunately, they might even have had the intention to hurt you, but behind that was still their desire to feel better in themselves.

It might look like this event was about you. The other person might even have been pointing their finger at you, telling you that it's all about you, but when you recognise that it wasn't really, that their driver was unconsciously to avoid their painful feelings of worthlessness, it drains away the toxic sense of victimhood.

Unwinding victimhood

Whenever you think of yourself as a victim, you put the other person into the role of a monster. As you start letting go, this view shifts. However, if you don't continue letting go and get right to the end of the process,

OUTSMART IMPOSTER SYNDROME

then a little resentment will always remain. Therefore, letting go may require several rounds as you slowly release the victimhood.

Releasing the victimhood often follows a predictable path:

> Monster –> Animal –> Human –> Like you –> See their unconditional worth

You might start at different points along this process. Sometimes, for example, you might not regard somebody as a monster who you blame. Rather, you might be disappointed in them as a human being, but still, you feel some distance between you and them.

It doesn't matter where you start from because the end result is a feeling of acceptance, forgiveness and gratitude towards them, regardless of how they feel towards you. Then you have become free. You have truly let go of that situation.

When you label the other person as a **monster**, then it becomes easy to blame them for the entire situation. Although their responsibility may be justified, the label of a monster implies they had bad intent.

Many people view others as an enemy or monster, but it locks in the negativity and sense of victimhood. It also locks the negative emotion-memory into the amygdala because the little sense of power from 'being right' undermines your capacity to let the situation go.

To get out of the victimhood trap, you need to separate the person (being) from their actions (doing). As we saw with unconditional worth in Chapter 5, a person is not their actions. Their worth is *not* what they do.

Once you've let go of seeing the other person as a monster, you may still feel a distance from them. You may still feel angry or hurt. You may still be judging them or seeing them as disgusting for what they've done or holding them in contempt. It is the view that they are beneath you and inferior.

At this stage, you will see them as an **animal**, that is, not quite human. Alternatively, you'll see them as threatening, which will continue to trigger the amygdala. Either way, you need to continue the letting-go process.

As you let go further, you begin to see the other person as a **human being**. This is where understanding their survival strategies comes in. You can understand why they did what they did. They have genuine reasons, however much you might disagree with those reasons. The other person may even be unaware of them. You also start to see that sometimes people make mistakes, poor choices or errors of judgement.

Although you can see them now as a human being, you may still feel cool towards the other person.

137

The distance remains. They are a faceless person that you can blame, so your victimhood persists.

As you go even further into letting go, you recognise that the other person is actually **like you**. You see the similarities between you more than the differences. Your ability to accept the other person increases.

Now take a deeper view. . . *if you had lived their life and had their exact experiences, skills and beliefs, you would have done the same thing they did.*

This is a mighty shift in terms of letting go. It is seeing that we're all human and we're all the same underneath. It acknowledges that we all make mistakes and have flaws. We all have past experiences that drive us.

Finally, you can **see their unconditional worth**. To fully accept the other person, you turn to the idea of conditional worth. As we saw in Chapter 5, people use the survival strategies of approval and praise, power, distraction, safety or drama when they get close to the painful feelings of unworthiness. If those don't work, they switch to compensating behaviours of attacking, acting like a victim, lying, running and clinging. Conditional worth drives all of these behaviours.

When you consider the other person's actions in this way, then real understanding occurs. You see them behaving from the pain of conditional worth.

You can understand that if they are verbally attacking you, it's because they're not getting their usual survival strategy fix. You can understand that they try to get that fix because, unconsciously, they feel their worth is not unconditional. Then you can understand that their stress and negative actions are driven by the need to escape the pain and feel a tiny bit better about themselves.

The survival strategies don't really help anyone to feel more worthy. They do just enough to keep people locked into replaying those patterns. People only continue using them because these negative coping strategies can feel better than nothing at all. That is, it's the best that they learned to do, and it was the best that they came up with as a child when they were growing up.

Understanding that people are doing the best they can with the resources they have is *not* excusing their actions. Nor does it remove the consequences of their negative actions.

For example, if you get caught speeding, then the natural consequence is that you have to pay a fine or take a driver's education course. The police officer doesn't need to be angry, disappointed, smug or blame you. They can just calmly write you a ticket because it's the natural consequence of breaking traffic laws.

Similarly, understanding why people do hurtful things doesn't mean that you let them off the hook.

It doesn't mean they have done the right thing, and it doesn't mean there won't be a consequence of their actions.

The difference is that you can enforce the consequence without having to have destructive negative internal feelings yourself. You become the calm, maybe even slightly bored traffic cop. You understand that people were doing the best they could with the *resources* that they had in that moment.

Those resources can be financial, material and physical. There are also mental resources that are reduced when people are in the fight, flight or freeze states. As we saw in Chapter 2, the IQ drops by thirteen points in such times of stress. People literally can't make such good decisions in that state.

Then there are emotional resources, such as how to be aware of and manage emotions. There are knowledge and skills on how to handle a particular situation. Finally, there are the beliefs that they've learned about the way that the world works.

When you see somebody behaving badly in a particular situation, such as verbally attacking somebody else, you now know that they lack skill in managing their feelings and are unable to express themselves better. They're simply doing the best that they've learned how to do. It's the best that they can do with the resources they have in the moment.

A positive perspective that works well here is that if the other person knew a better way of doing something, and had the resources to allow them to do so, they would do it that way. If you can view the target of your letting-go process from the perspective of 'we are all doing the best we can with the resources we have', it becomes your superpower. You can now let go of your sense of victimhood and become neutral towards them.

7: Feel

Now you understand the mechanisms behind the other person's actions, and the habits of behaviour they had developed. When you see the strange, incomprehensible, destructive things that people do as being driven by pain they're not aware of, it all makes sense and you can start to have compassion for them.

How terrible must it be for them to be so reactive or hurtful and not see other options for their behaviour? Not to have the skills to deal with their stress, anger or fear? How difficult must it be for them to live with being constantly triggered by their environment? To have their emotions dictated by what happens around them? It's a painful, difficult, stressful and lonely way to live their life.

If you don't rush this, then you'll feel relieved as you realise that their actions don't define *your* worth.

They were just reacting to their own internal pain. Your emotions towards them shifts to compassion. Even though the facts of the past have not changed in any way, you're no longer locked into toxic victimhood and only one (negative) interpretation of the event.

8: Celebrate

The last step is to generate even more positive emotion to complete the change in your amygdala. The negative emotional charge is released and you can finally relax.

To achieve this closure, imagine feeling grateful for having had the other person as a teacher in your life. They've supplied an example that you can use to develop your letting-go skills, at the very least. You have learned to forgive them and accept their humanity, which sets *you* free. You understand that it's not about you and the hurt feeling starts to dissolve. Their actions are no longer triggering a sense of you being worthless.

Together, compassion and gratitude raise your positive emotions higher than the neutral. Experiencing these warm emotions while still remembering the facts of the previously painful event has changed the way that your amygdala processes it. The amygdala ceases to define it as dangerous. This means that you won't automatically fall into a rut of negative thinking the next time you're reminded of the event.

Additionally, celebrate this shift. Jump into finally feeling free from the event, congratulate yourself for this big change, feel excitement for your future free from it haunting you. A strong emotion of celebration fosters your feeling of calm and being cooperative.

Gone for good

The letting-go process we've explored here is a permanent shift in how you view this one event. It is not a mindset exercise that you need to repeat over and over. If you get to feeling compassion and gratitude, and truly caring for the other person, then the work is done.

In bringing yourself to this deep level of acceptance and compassion for them, you shift your overall memory of the event into the positive. It feels light and calm. You might even laugh, like James, and be surprised and delighted by this shift.

Emotional intelligence

When you master this letting-go process, you naturally increase your emotional intelligence because you are separating a person's actions from their worth as a human being. It naturally increases your respect and tolerance for other people, which carries over to all your relationships and benefits them immensely.

You understand why people do the ugly, hurtful, clumsy things that they do, and you understand that it's the same driver for us all. You stop being a victim, blown around like a leaf in the wind by other people's behaviour. When you can see their humanity and all their flaws, that sets *you* free.

The letting-go process described here is a hugely powerful tool to change your amygdala response to one event. Even by itself, it is therapeutic. However, we have not yet accomplished the goal of eliminating imposter syndrome and developing unconditional worth. For this, we need to use the letting-go process in a systematic, targeted manner, as you will see next.

SEVEN
Join The Dots

We've now explored a powerful set of tools which have great benefits individually. However, your goal here is to eliminate imposter syndrome, and the ultimate solution to that is to change the worth belief from conditional to unconditional. When you remove the fuel of conditional worth, the fire of imposter syndrome simply goes out.

In this chapter, we combine these tools in a systematic way that maximises the positive change you can create. We'll dive deeper into the neural mechanism of belief change, look at the individual emotion-memories and their collective contribution to conditional worth, and then examine how to create unconditional worth.

Neurochemical secrets

While neuroscientists explored the brain's ability to change, neuroplasticity, it became clear that an adult's brain is less plastic or changeable than a baby's. This makes sense, because the adult brain has a well-established internal model of the world that has proven its efficacy. If the adult brain had the plasticity of a young child's, a lifetime of essential learnings could easily be 'overwritten' and the precious information lost.

This difference between child and adult brains is why many neuroscientists in the 1950s thought the adult brain to be fixed. This idea is echoed in the common saying 'You can't teach an old dog new tricks.'

Neuroplasticity in an adult's brain solves the problem of overwriting a good internal model by being selective, and only certain areas of the brain update. You can learn to scuba-dive while on holiday, for example, whereas the ability to learn a new language with native fluency disappears after the age of seven.

A key for neuroplasticity is the release of a neurochemical called acetylcholine, which signals to emotion-memories to become receptive to change. Most areas of an adult's brain have a neurochemical inhibitor present that dampens the influence of acetylcholine, and so prevents change, but certain areas do not have that inhibitor and so remain adaptable to change.

One of these adaptable areas is the amygdala. This makes sense, because throughout your life, you can encounter new dangers, which your amygdala needs to be able to learn about to continue to keep you safe.

Thus, to change your amygdala response to dangers past and present, you need to release acetylcholine in the brain. This can be done via any of three mechanisms: relevance, surprise or strong emotion.[51]

Relevance

Relevance means that the current situation is significant to your brain. That is, it's either a danger or a reward. When experimental rats learned a difficult manoeuvre to access a treat, for example, they remember it the next time and are faster at reaching the reward. However, if they were injected with an acetylcholine inhibitor, they did not remember how they accessed the food, so were just as slow to reach it as they had been the first time.

Similar experiments with mild electric shocks showed the same results, using pain rather than reward, and the memories could only be formed only when acetylcholine was present. It was the **relevance** of the pain or reward to the rat's survival that stimulated the brain to release acetylcholine.

Surprise

The brain also releases acetylcholine in an unexpected situation. Recall that the brain needs to predict the future as well as possible, but a surprise is new information that does not match its predictions. This requires the internal model to be revised, in case it is a danger or reward situation to learn from. Thus, **surprise** releases acetylcholine and gives the amygdala the ability to modify the emotion-memory.

Strong emotion

Similarly, strong emotions are an indication of potential danger or survival/social reward. Acetylcholine is released in the presence of these emotions, whether positive or negative. The amygdala will either change the emotion-memory or reinforce it, depending on which emotions are experienced.

Strong negative emotions, such as fear or anger, release stress neurochemicals of cortisol and adrenaline. The acetylcholine makes the emotion-memory changeable, and if it is a fear memory, then the neurochemicals from strong negative emotions will reinforce or 'reconsolidate' it, and no change will be made.

Strong positive emotions release neurochemicals of serotonin, dopamine, endorphins and oxytocin. These neurochemicals block the reconsolidation of the fear memory, that is, they result in changing the fear memory so that the amygdala no longer defines the situation as a threat.[52]

This cocktail of neurochemicals appears to be the natural mechanism for the brain to continually refine its internal model in the amygdala. Like any savvy cocktail maker, we can concoct our own mix of neurochemicals to achieve our aim.[53] We can deliberately stimulate acetylcholine to switch on change, and then tune into specific emotions to guide the direction of that change. That is, these additional neurochemicals determine whether the fear memory is extinguished or enhanced. It gives us a powerful means to deliberately adjust the brain's automatic reaction to the events around us.

The letting-go process outlined in the previous chapter was originally developed based on the combination of thousands of hours of coaching focused on conditional worth with as many hours of neurofeedback targeting brain changes. These two approaches had been developed by trial and error, without any knowledge of the mechanism that caused the positive results.

The effectiveness of these two approaches can be explained by the understanding of the neurochemical interactions. That understanding was then used to further refine the letting-go process by removing steps that didn't have a neuroscience basis and adding in new ones that did. The resulting process which is presented in this book is consistently effective to permanently change individual emotion-memories.

Let's take a look at the letting-go process from the viewpoint of these neurochemicals.

The neurochemical dance

The carefully choreographed dance of the letting-go process is a systematic way to create the right neurochemical environment to allow permanent emotion-memory change in the amygdala.

The first step, to **choose** a specific situation, uses *relevance* to release acetylcholine. You are selecting an emotion-memory with significance for you. That significance can be your desire to change this one emotion-memory or the understanding that this one step is taking you closer to your greater goal of eliminating imposter syndrome. Either way, it is important to you.

When you **decide** to let go of the situation, this is more *relevance* because you are determined to make this change. You're focused on making a change that you see as beneficial.

As you **imagine** charging the person with their actions as in a courtroom, you bring more *relevance* by narrowing your attention to this one event. You've now taken three steps of relevance, each of which releases acetylcholine, priming your brain to change this emotion-memory.

However, if you were unmotivated, indifferent or even half-hearted about this process, then it would not register as relevant. This means that the acetylcholine would not be released, and so no change would occur. Thus, being motivated to do this work is required to make it effective.

In the next step, you **access** the *strong emotions* that you had during the event, and these are negative emotions. If you continued to sit with these negative emotions, your system would release cortisol and adrenaline as you re-experience these feelings. This, in the presence of acetylcholine, would reconsolidate the fear memory and lock it in further.

However, in letting go, you don't stay with the negative emotions for long. You just dip into them to create the greatest contrast with the positive emotions that will follow.

You quickly **find** the gift and feel positive emotions for that. This rapid flip between negative and positive emotions creates *surprise* and releases even more acetylcholine.[54] However, if you feel deeply into the positivity of the gift, you will also engage *strong emotions* and make the change even more effective.

To **understand** the other person is an intellectual step rather than an emotional one. However, it often leads to a sense of relief and a softening of the judgement towards the other person, adding more positive emotions into the mix.

The next step, to **feel compassion**, is absolutely generating *strong emotion*, specifically strong positive emotion. This releases more acetylcholine, while the positive emotions release neurochemicals such as serotonin and dopamine. These switch the amygdala's assessment of the situation from threat to non-threat. Finally, the **celebrate** step engages *strong emotions* again, having the same effect as before, but adding neurochemicals of endorphins and oxytocin, which generate feelings of calm, kindness, safety and cooperation.[55]

Once you've finished letting go, you need to stop focusing on this situation and let it pass. Ideally go and do something entirely different. This allows the neurochemicals to gently settle to background levels, effectively sealing the change in place.

The change experienced is a completely permanent memory change, that is, the negative emotional charge of the emotion-memory is dissipated.[56] Recall James's surprised delight at how differently he felt about the situation after his first letting-go.

If you do not evoke enough compassion and positive emotion in the last steps, you may not get the complete transformation. Indeed, it is common for people to have to repeat the same letting-go a few times when they first learn the process, until they can generate strong enough compassion to complete the change. As they master the process, they get better and faster at it, and then once is enough to get the full transformation.

Because this is a change in the amygdala, the new perspective of the event is at an unconscious level. That is, the change is not only permanent, but you do not have to continually remind yourself to think positively about the situation. It comes about effortlessly without your conscious attention.

Up to this point, the letting-go work has been to change the emotion-memory of one isolated event. Next, we look at how we can use this powerful process strategically to target the belief of conditional worth.

Change conditional worth

When the brain first develops a belief, it tests this belief in different situations, looking for proof that it is correct for the internal model. It updates the belief depending on what it finds, via the neurochemical interactions mentioned above. As the brain gets more proof from more confirming experiences, the belief becomes more valid for the internal model.

I see beliefs much like old-fashioned gobstopper or jawbreaker candies. These were small round cores with layers of coloured hard-candy shell added. The more layers, the larger the ball got. The result was solid and was too hard to bite or crunch. The only way to eat it was to dissolve the layers slowly.

Confirming experiences

Similarly, a small core belief can have multiple layers of confirming experiences. The more layers there are, the more the core belief is 'locked' into place. That is, it's held to be true by the brain.

Every new experience either confirms or contradicts the belief. For example, with the imposter behaviour of deflecting praise, you assume others are wrong, mistaken, fooled or after something when they praise you. You simply don't believe that you deserve the praise because it contradicts your brain's internal model that you're not good enough.

Conditional worth has been seen as difficult to change because it is a deep-seated identity-level belief with a lifetime of confirming experiences. However, we now know that such change is possible provided we use the right techniques.

Unconditional worth can be described as having deep self-acceptance, where we are not judging or criticising ourselves, but instead have understanding and compassion towards ourselves. However, the vast majority of us have instead held the conditional worth belief all our lives, which means we have many layers of experiences that seem to confirm conditional worth. We can't just jump straight into having deep self-acceptance.

The way to get there is to start small and to start with other people. That is, we first learn to accept others exactly as they are. Warts and all, as the saying goes. We can achieve this deep acceptance only when the other person, their actions and their history with us do not trigger our nervous system. That is, our amygdala ceases to react to them as a threat.

Thus, the first step in developing our own unconditional worth is to change the amygdala's reaction to others, which is where letting go works so beautifully. After starting with letting go for others regarding small situations, we build up to more significant events, changing emotion-memories one at a time.

Memory association

Does this mean we have to work through a letting-go process for every painful experience? Thankfully, no. Memories are stored by association in the brain, that is, groups of related events or ideas.[57] This means that every time we let go of the emotional pain of one small event, the emotional pain of related events is released slightly too.

A cluster of associated memories is like air filling a balloon: release some of the air and the whole balloon gets smaller. In the same way, release one painful memory and the overall pain from this group of memories reduces. The number required to make a significant difference is surprisingly small. Doing the letting-go process fifteen to twenty times will create a massive shift.

Remove the proof

Because memories are associative, each letting-go you complete chips away at your locked-in conditional worth. You choose small emotion-memories that have formed the 'evidence' of your conditional worth and let go for these, then slowly build to more significant memories.

You must start with small situations because you need to remain in the fellow state throughout the process. If an emotion-memory is too highly charged, too locked into your amygdala, then your nervous system will get triggered. Your brain cannot make positive changes in this state and the process will not be effective. If this happens, you need to get calm again and try with a smaller, easier situation. Remember also that this process is unsuitable for significant trauma, PTSD or mental illness without qualified help.

Donna wanted to do some letting go regarding her ex-business partner as they were dissolving their partnership.

She found she got too triggered when thinking of the 'big' conflicts around client disputes and financial anomalies. She could not let go of the situation, nor feel compassion towards her ex-business partner.

She tried letting go for a smaller event, but that was also too hard, so she instead focused on a tiny irritation. He would frequently forget to save his expenses receipts. It had exasperated her throughout their partnership and had created an unnecessary workload. The situation, however, was small enough that she could let it go all the way to compassion.

Once she let go of the receipts issue, then it was easy for Donna to step up to progressively larger disagreements until she could fully let go of the biggest disputes.

As you do this work, you naturally start to apply the freedom framework we looked at in Chapter 5 to all people you interact with. You become more accepting of them. You are not condoning their actions, but you are accepting that they are human, make mistakes and are doing the best they can.

Develop unconditional worth

In doing this letting-go work, you begin to realise that one person's worth is unconditional. As you do it for more and more people, you see that everybody's worth is unconditional. You are connecting with the essential equality of all humans.

This alone is an amazing shift. It changes how you interact with everyone around you. You feel calmer and more resilient, regardless of how people behave. This reduces other people's influence on how you think of yourself in the face of their approval or disapproval. You now see their negative opinions as an expression of their pain and having nothing to do with your worth. As a result, you feel more confident that you can handle whatever comes your way.

Now you are ready to move on and let go of your judgement and criticism of yourself. You use exactly the same letting-go process, but imagine yourself as the 'accused'. You charge yourself with actions that you have judged, blamed or criticised yourself for.

Again, you start with the small events and build to larger ones. You are smoothly unravelling all of the inputs to your belief of being less than fully worthy. You gradually develop deep self-acceptance and compassion for yourself. Finally, you start to feel good enough and a solid sense of your own unconditional worth emerges.

James followed the letting-go process to the letter. He started with small irritations that still bothered him: the stranger who had keyed his new car, the supplier who had missed their promised deadline, the neighbour who built a house extension that put James's garden in shadow and more. These small events familiarised him with the process and gave him confidence with following it.

James moved on to more significant situations: the ridiculous argument with his brother eight years ago, one teacher's hurtful comment in school and the ex-colleague who undermined him in front of the boss. As he let go and forgave each one, James felt lighter every time. Things from his past that had haunted him for years were released, relaxed and soothed, one by one.

Then James came to an event he'd thought impossible to let go of when he first started this work.

In James's first executive role, his position had also been new and the scope of his work was still being defined. One colleague, Brian, seemed unhappy with James's appointment and kept trying to step in and take over, even though Brian would not have been able to take on James's work too, there was simply too much to be done. Brian was also a bully who frequently argued with and criticised James.

In James's first executive planning meeting with his eleven colleagues and the CEO, he was outlining his work and plans for the year ahead when Brian interrupted. He picked apart James's presentation, accused him of missing the most vital part and verbally attacked him, calling him an idiot who should never have been hired.

Mortified, James looked to his CEO, Sean, who had already approved those plans. Sean said nothing and looked away. James turned to three colleagues who he'd become friends with, but they too stayed silent. Another colleague took

Brian's side and argued for a redefinition of the role. No one stepped in to back up James.

James felt shocked, betrayed, confused and alone. He quit soon after and found himself a better position with a supportive boss and peers. However, the pain, humiliation and anger stayed with James whenever he thought about that occasion. Even years later, this old event made him second-guess himself and hold back from putting forward ideas. It made him less willing to trust others, too. It also explains why James was so shaken by his current boss's criticism, which we saw in Chapter 2 triggered the freeze state. It was an echo of this past event.

James started with letting go for Sean for not stepping in and correcting Brian. He now understood that Sean's survival strategy was praise and approval and that he tended to avoid conflict. James realised that Sean had never been able to handle Brian very well and clearly felt helpless.

Sean also seemed to take a lot of time off, likely running from what must have seemed to be an impossible situation. James felt compassion for him and saw that Sean didn't have the knowledge or skills to handle Brian. Sean's inability to intervene in the planning meeting was not about James. It was not personal and had nothing to do with James's work.

Then James let go for his colleagues who didn't speak up and support him. Looking back, he remembered how shocked they had appeared. They were also intimidated by Brian's outburst and didn't want to be targets themselves.

Recalling comments they had made before, James saw that they had been bullied by Brian in the past too. He also realised that they hadn't known enough details to know who was right, either, so they had no strong grounds to back him up. James understood their difficult position and that their inaction was about them, not him. He felt compassion for their position.

Next, James came to letting go for Brian's attack in that meeting. James saw that bullying to get his way was the only tool that Brian had when dealing with people. He had a reputation for being difficult to work with, which isolated him in the company and meant he had very little support, so Brian would have been feeling vulnerable and unable to use his typical power survival strategy. When Brian felt isolated and helpless, then his compensating behaviour was to attack. No wonder he went after James in such a public way.

When James saw that Brian's attack was not about him, but about Brian, he started to feel sorry for Brian for having such limited ways of interacting. James realised that if Brian had known a more effective way to feel included, supported and strong, then he would have used it.

Lastly, James forgave himself for his own behaviour. What he had said and not said, and for quitting, which he had previously felt ashamed of and branded himself a failure for. James accepted that he had done the best that he could see at the time. He stopped feeling like a victim and instead viewed himself with compassion and acceptance.

Breaking down this big, significant, distressing experience into separate smaller experiences and letting go for each one individually turned it around completely for James. He no longer felt anxious or angry when he thought about it. He no longer took it personally, as he could see this was a group of people doing their best to deal with a high-stress situation. James had finally forgiven Sean, his ex-colleagues, Brian and himself. This event no longer defined him and his behaviour, and he was free from its influence at last.

Letting go of this situation and several others related to conditional worth meant James started to accept himself and feel unconditionally worthy. From here, he became more comfortable with stepping into the spotlight. He seized opportunities rather than avoid risks, and spoke up expressing his thoughts and ideas. It was effortless confidence and forgetting to doubt himself. He felt excited to make a contribution and lead in the way he'd always hoped he could lead.

This is not therapy

Although letting go for these situations is significant and therapeutic, it is *not* therapy.

Neuroscientists call therapy 'cognitive reappraisal'. That is, to become aware of specific past painful events or relationships and reframe how you consciously think about them. (Therapy is also designed to help people move from mental dysfunction to normal functioning, but that's not our focus here.)

By contrast, neuroscientists would call the process of change used in letting go 'blocking the reconsolidation' of specific emotion-memories. That is, creating a permanent shift using the innate brain mechanisms that update the amygdala and change what is considered to be a threat at the unconscious level.

As a further step, the work presented here targets the unconscious conditional worth belief stored in the amygdala by letting go for a *collection* of emotion-memories. The aim is not to resolve one painful situation, but rather to systematically resolve a series of events, using them as stepping stones that all together resolve the conditional worth belief.

This is an important distinction, as each letting-go, from the very smallest, is a crucial step in our overall goal. Each letting-go has *relevance* to the overall process, and so the brain releases the acetylcholine that makes the change possible.

Imagine training to lift 100kg weights at the gym. You start with 5kg weights to learn how to lift correctly and safely. Then you progress to heavier weights until you reach your goal. You don't mind starting small with 5kg weights because this is important to the process, and you would injure yourself if you went straight to the heaviest ones.

However, if you did not have the goal to lift heavier weights, then you'd be unlikely to want to lift 5kg weights all the time. There would be little gain and therefore no relevance, which means you'd struggle to find the motivation.

In the same way, you need to learn the letting-go process for minor situations. If you were to start on more difficult situations, which would trigger your nervous system, like a muscle injury, then it would hinder your progress.

However, merely letting go for one minor situation would not make a big enough change in your life to motivate you to do it. It would not have enough relevance to you to release acetylcholine. Thus a smaller letting-go is practice and skill-development for larger ones, and the ultimate goal is to change from conditional to unconditional worth so as to finally eliminate imposter syndrome. This goal gives you a great reason to do even the smallest letting-go.

Although elements of letting-go are seen in lots of therapeutic approaches, it is its systematic application towards the specific goal of unconditional worth that sets this process apart. As you release the emotional charge regarding the events that previously confirmed conditional worth, your brain has less and less evidence that the belief is true. In fact, the process links positive emotions that confirm unconditional worth instead.

As you apply the process further, your brain receives more and more evidence that unconditional worth is true for other people. This allows you to feel a deep level of acceptance for others. You then progress to developing your own unconditional worth and a deep self-acceptance, regardless of situations around you. You have finally separated your actions from your worth.

Emotional intelligence

When you master letting go like this, you naturally develop high emotional intelligence as you are able to separate a person's actions from their worth as a human being. This automatically raises your respect and tolerance for other people without you even thinking about it. It carries over to all your relationships and benefits them immensely.

You understand why people do the ugly, hurtful, clumsy or accidental things that they do, and you understand that it's the same driver for all of us. You stop feeling like a victim blown around like a leaf in the wind by other people's behaviour and opinions. When you can see their humanity and all their flaws, that sets *you* free.

You can even find yourself going through the process in real time while you're in the middle of a difficult situation. This means that you can clear the past, deal gracefully with current difficulties and have confidence that you can handle further difficulties easily too.

Close the loop

Let's come full circle back to outsmarting imposter syndrome and eliminating it for good. All the elements covered in this book are essential, as is the order in which they are done, because it is a systematic process rather than a list of techniques.

You first learned the neuroregulation tools to calm your nervous system and access the fellow state. This means that you're able to reset yourself back into the fellow state whenever you get triggered. You also learned how to manage your time and energy in your work and personal life so that fewer situations activate your nervous system. Thus, you're able to handle the day-to-day challenges with greater ease. Then you developed a plan to relax the imposter behaviours. This is all managing imposter syndrome and breaking the cycle of its symptoms.

Next, in working through the letting-go process multiple times for specific events, you have removed the threat triggers from your amygdala. This allows you to remain calmly detached yet fully present in the face of situations that previously triggered you. This happens at an entirely unconscious level, which makes it automatic and effortless. You have developed uncon-scious neuroregulation, that is, you don't have to actively think about it.

In this way, the physiological stress symptom of imposter syndrome melts away and you become more consistently calm and in the high-performance fellow state. When you feel calmer in this way, your impulse to engage in imposter behaviours is reduced significantly. The fuel to these fires is gone and you no longer need these coping patterns.

Even if you still experienced a residual habit of these behaviours, your new-found levels of self-acceptance mean that you won't beat yourself up, criticise or judge yourself for it. Instead, you understand and feel com-passion for yourself. Free from that self-judgement, you can quickly course correct. The gradual expo-sure process from Chapter 4 now works exceptionally well for you to retrain yourself out of the habit of those behaviours.

Finally, the imposter syndrome thinking has flipped entirely. You've gone from automatic self-criticism to automatic self-acceptance. That is, you have achieved unconditional worth. You're not trying to talk yourself into thinking positively, you just do it effortlessly. You have forgotten to doubt yourself and a solid sense of your comfort, confidence and belonging blossoms.

From here, you shift the way in which you lead and mentor others at work. The basis for your leadership has become good neuroregulation, high emotional intelligence and a natural respect for and acceptance of yourself and others.

Let's now look at how unconditional worth naturally changes the way that you lead.

EIGHT
Worth-based Leadership

*A*s *James settled into his new belief in his unconditional worth, it changed how he led his team. Imposter syndrome had previously made him doubt whether he was a good leader. He had worried that he might not have the right qualities, traits or personality for it.*

This echoes the question of whether leaders are born or made, which has been debated for centuries by great thinkers from ancient Chinese sages and Greek philosophers to the present day. It has given rise to a whole slew of personality profiling tests to identify a good leader. There are 100,000+ books on leadership available today. In many of them, you'll see a subtle statement of conditional worth.

Actually, now that you know what to look for, it's not so subtle. The authors tell you to *be* a good leader, *be* authentic, *be* creative, *be* resilient, *be* decisive, *be* empathic and to *be* many more things too. This suggests that you (hence your worth) and your actions are one.

These books don't differentiate between the self and actions, which is hardly surprising because it is a blind spot for society in general. Unfortunately, being told that you need to be different implies that who you are is not good enough, and that you should be better than you are. It feeds into the imposter syndrome thought patterns.

I'm firmly in the 'leaders are made' camp. Great leadership comes from skills, motivation, awareness and consciously held beliefs.

Leadership requires skills to be taught, whether in childhood or in the workplace. Businesses are often great at training people in technical skills, but less good about training for skills in managing human interactions. This is because leadership is too often considered to be part of our personality rather than a skill that we can learn and refine.

Your leadership is directed by the beliefs you hold, your awareness of yourself and others, and your ability to manage yourself and your relationships with others. In this chapter, we'll explore different aspects of leadership and how to apply what you've learned about beliefs, conditional worth and imposter syndrome from this book.

Understanding your team

One of James's team, Tom, had a problematic communication style. Rather than confront issues when they were minor, Tom would wait until he'd worked himself up into a storm of anger, and then blame and complain loudly. It happened every three months or so, and James had always felt trapped, uncomfortable and manipulated by it.

James cared about his team, and Tom's dramatic outbursts made him feel that he was failing as a leader. An outburst would keep James awake that night, worrying about whether he was doing the right thing for Tom or that he was not a good enough leader.

One day, Tom came into James's office to complain about something new. Because of his work to eliminate imposter syndrome and develop unconditional worth, James responded differently to Tom's outburst this time. He sat and listened calmly without getting dragged into the drama of the old pattern.

Tom had a reputation for being a difficult employee in the company, but James could now clearly see how Tom used the drama survival strategy together with acting like a victim and attacking compensating behaviours. He understood that this was just Tom's style of speaking up for himself, destructive though it was.

Understanding that this was the best Tom had learned, James no longer took his outburst as a personal attack. In fact, James felt a little sorry for Tom that he didn't know a better way to express his needs. In their meeting this time, James was present, listened kindly and afterwards made two quick phone calls to remedy the problem. He then went on with his work, relaxed and focused for another productive afternoon.

Tom hadn't changed at all, but James had. He'd let go of the beliefs that would have previously sucked him in and turned Tom's drama into a crisis. As a result of his new insight, James also started exploring training options to help Tom improve his communication skills.

When you understand why your team members behave the way they do – that it comes from their beliefs, how they've learned to behave and that's the best they can do – then you don't take their stress personally. This means your nervous system is not triggered by their behaviour and you stay calm. Just like James, you naturally have compassion for their difficulty and want to help. You will find yourself doing more mentoring and team development because you want your team members to be happy in their work.

You are not making their reactions their fault or blaming them, but you are not abdicating responsibility for your contribution to their stress either. When someone is upset, you don't take it personally any more, but you *do* take their complaints seriously and try to make their working environment better. This includes looking at your own style of leadership and your skills, if necessary.

Micro-managing, for example, often comes from perfectionism and a desire to maintain control (power or safety survival strategy). When you develop your unconditional worth, then you become more relaxed and less likely to micromanage. You will be able to focus on others more, rather than worrying about yourself, and you will spot signs of stress in your team more easily. Then, for example, if you're told that you're micro-managing, you won't take it personally, and you can look calmly at your behaviour and get additional training if you need it.

Communicating effectively

How you say something is as important as what you say. It reveals your beliefs and feelings, which are communicated in hundreds of ways through body language, tone of voice, breathing patterns, facial micro-expressions and more.[58]

The 2013 ESADE Business School study, mentioned in Chapter 2, concluded that transformational leaders are those who have the ability to regulate their nervous system *and those of others* better than most. How do you regulate some else's nervous system? The amygdala takes cues of safety from other people

173

as well as from the environment. A sudden gasp in a crowded restaurant will cause heads to turn instantly. The gasp communicates surprise and possible danger, so everyone will want to see what the danger is in case they need to take action to save themselves.

When you're a leader, a stressed nervous system state will communicate to your team that there is danger, which will in turn activate their nervous systems. Everyone becomes agitated and their own stress behaviours emerge. Suddenly, your calm, rational meeting becomes heated as everyone loses IQ, creativity, the ability to think clearly, and the willingness to be bold.

In the same way, when you maintain a calm nervous system, it communicates to your team members that there is no danger here and that they are safe. Creativity, decisiveness and smart solutions are a natural by-product of a calmer internal landscape.

As a leader, you are helping to regulate your team's nervous systems as well as your own. The fewer triggers you have, the easier this is to do. When you develop unconditional worth, it becomes effortless and automatic.

High-performance environment

In a high-performance team, you have a challenge or problem to solve, usually with time pressure and a large workload. This is a classic environment trigger for imposter syndrome.

However, you are unlikely to spot it in your team. The people you think are handling things well, those you think would never have imposter syndrome, can be the ones who are struggling the most. As a leader, you need to ensure that your team's environment is optimal for results, productivity and sustainability. That is, not exhausting and burning them out.

Keeping an eye on the workload and prioritisation will help at the most basic level. Not asking for help or not saying no can be detrimental habits adopted by someone with imposter syndrome. To counter that, create a work environment where it's OK not only to ask for and accept help, but to proactively offer help too.

Creating a culture of sustainable high performance also means supporting the team in managing their time, even at the highest levels. One lovely work practice I've seen recently is to schedule meetings for fifty-five minutes instead of the standard one hour. Sticking to that time limit gives everyone a five-minute break before the next one. This simple practice makes back-to-back meetings far more manageable, especially in today's hybrid work environment.

Remember that the peak-performance flow state occurs when people are working at just 4% above their capacity. Short bursts beyond that are the normal ebb and flow of a dynamic environment, but continuously working beyond that can lead to exhaustion, burnout and people quitting. If you, as the leader of a high-performance team, focus on this metric, then it will pay dividends.

Learn from Tom Blomfield's experience of burnout mentioned in Chapter 3. Treat the potential loss of a key team member as a high-risk scenario and create plans to mitigate that risk. Don't simply assume that because your team members are such star performers that they can pick up another person's work without consequences. These consequences will be their own energy and performance, and can tip them over towards exhaustion and burnout too.

High status, high-performance companies are now starting to pay attention to their 'legacy culture' of overworking. It is a significant problem regarding exhaustion, burnout, lack of mental wellbeing and reduced employee retention. Unfortunately, this overwork has been considered a necessary consequence of a demanding workplace. It's been this way for years, so the culture has normalised it.

It is essential to recognise that a nervous system activated by stress and overwork decreases an individual's capacity to perform. The result is that the legacy overwork culture creates, in effect, not a high-performance environment but a mediocre one.

Toxic environment

A toxic work environment can have devastating effects on wellbeing, creativity, decision making, productivity and performance, as well as job satisfaction and contribution. Deal with bullying behaviour as a priority. You now know how it affects people's nervous systems and creates stress not only for those being bullied, but also for everyone who witnesses it.

I often hear that a top performer in terms of output, sales etc is allowed to get away with inappropriate behaviour because their results are so good. You can now understand how their behaviour leads to a hostile or aggressive workplace, which will have a negative effect on everyone's nervous system. Even though this one person is currently getting the top results, they are actually creating a poor performance environment around them.

Allowing such prima-donna behaviour to go unchecked can degrade the overall team dynamic. Much is lost in the short term in performance and in the long term where unhappy team members leave, increasing the knock-on costs of rehiring and training.

Managing survival strategies

When you're regulating your nervous system well, your amygdala is not triggered, so there is no threat. You're communicating that there is no danger present. There has been plenty of discussion in books and the media in recent years about creating a psychologically safe workplace, one in which people can feel comfortable expressing themselves without fear of reprisal. Good nervous system regulation creates *physiological safety*, that is, the brain recognises that there is no physical danger in the environment. The impact of physiological safety at an unconscious level is perhaps more significant than we could have previously imagined.

Using the framework for understanding others that we examined in Chapter 5, you can proactively assess which survival strategies are being used by your team members, colleagues and leaders. As you now know, these are the behaviours that come out when people are stressed, in a crisis or under excessive pressure. You can use that information to choose what you could do to help them feel physiologically safe. What will not trigger their nervous system and instead keep them in the fellow state?

If someone on your team uses the survival strategy of **power**, then they feel most comfortable when they are in control of people and decisions. Feeling in control means they feel strong and safe. That is, they feel unsafe when they are out of control.

If they can't gain control, then they may move to their compensating behaviours such as attacking, which often goes with the power survival strategy. When you see someone who is attacking from this perspective, you can then have compassion for them. It's a horrible feeling to have only power and attacking as a way to handle a situation.

What can you do to help them? Someone with the power survival strategy will always like choices. Offer whatever choices you can and they will immediately feel a little safer. Even if you ask, 'Do you want the bad news or shall I lie to you?' in a relaxed, light manner, you're still giving them a choice. That choice will make them feel safer even when the news is indeed bad.

For people using the **praise/approval** survival strategy, they feel most stressed by disapproval and criticism. Here, you can make sure that you acknowledge their work, results etc. In conflicts, often the kindness or courtesy of praise and acknowledgement is the first thing to go and discussions can devolve into mutual attack or criticism.

When you're able to regulate your nervous system so that you're not using compensating behaviours, then you can make sure that all discussions, even difficult ones, have a strong element of respect and acknowledgement for the other person. This will help the person with the praise survival strategy feel safe and able to regulate their own nervous system.

With the **distraction** survival strategy, people will feel overwhelmed by a difficult situation and seek to escape the real emotional pain of it. You are unlikely to see their escapism in a work environment as they're probably doing distracting behaviours at home. But you might notice their compensating behaviour of withdrawal or running. The team member who sits back and doesn't engage in the meeting, for example, may be feeling overwhelmed. Here, time and space for them to get calm again will be helpful. If it's a long meeting, take a short fresh-air break and allow them a little escape that will soothe their stress.

In a similar way to power, the **safety** strategy is also about control, but it is control of the environment. These people seek to try to minimise any surprises. Last-minute changes and unplanned events will make them feel unsafe. You can help manage their survival strategy by keeping their schedule as stable as possible and giving them plenty of notice for changes to it.

With the **drama** survival strategy, this person feels safest when they have attention and feel unsafe when they are lost in the background. When triggered, they can be too outspoken or disruptive in discussions. To feel safe, they need to feel included and appreciated. Unfortunately, their behaviour when they don't feel this sense of safety often drives other people away, who then withdraw their approval or attention. This makes the person feel even less safe. Simple steps like making sure you make eye contact with them as you look around the room, and refer to their ideas if appropriate, will help them feel included and, therefore, safe.

Managing people's survival strategies in this way is not manipulation. It is being able to recognise what different people need to feel physiologically safe. This helps them to feel more like they belong, enjoy their work and be more productive, creative and cooperative in the fellow state.

The motivation here is to help your team members from a place of understanding and compassion. Their survival strategies are *not* their personalities. In fact, they are rarely even conscious behaviours, so there is nothing to blame or judge people for. This is the best they can do with the resources they have in the moment.

Unconditional worth principles

When you bring in a few principles of unconditional worth, you can make a big positive change in your team. For example, competition can be a fun, exciting motivator when done well. Framing any win based on the achievement and not the worth of the person makes the difference here. The principle is that someone may be better at doing something, but that does not make them a better person than anyone else.

When you reward and praise, always make sure you praise the action and not the person so that you reinforce unconditional worth. Make their success about what they achieved rather than who they are.

Praise in itself is not the solution to imposter syndrome in your team, however. With imposter syndrome, people may not even believe your praise is genuine or true. Instead, they could feel like you are one more person they have fooled.

If you suspect that is the case, then rather than praising their contribution, ask the team member what *they* thought of their results. What did they enjoy about this project? What was the most satisfying part? What part of it would they like to do again? What did they learn from it?

Here, you are stepping back from being the judge of them (as a person) and allowing them to discover their own authority.

Belonging

Feeling like you don't belong is such a common feature of imposter syndrome that it is important to address it proactively. Understand that people compare themselves to one another constantly, and use the differences they find as evidence that they don't belong. Regardless of whether someone outwardly looks identical to their peers or completely unlike them, they can always find 'evidence' of ways in which they are different, and this feeds into a feeling of not belonging.

You can break this pattern by focusing on similarities rather than differences in your communication, and encourage others to do so too.

Role model

Every leader is a role model for their team. Children learn from copying their parents, team members learn from copying their leaders. A leader sets the tone, models behaviour and demonstrates the beliefs that they hold.

Carlos, a Chief Technical Officer with a team of eighty people, told me about his exhaustion. His over-preparing and perfectionism meant that he worked extremely long hours. Close to burnout, he was keen to learn how to change this pattern.

Carlos also observed that seven of his team members had had time off for burnout within the previous six months. His long hours and never switching off did not go unnoticed. He was modelling the behaviour and his team members were following suit.

He was, in effect, communicating that there is danger in the work environment (activated nervous system) and that the solution is to work long hours. When Carlos changed the driver for his behaviour, then he was more relaxed, which communicated safety to his team. He stopped working excessive hours and sending late-night work emails, and his whole team breathed a sigh of relief.

Effortless leadership

The principles and examples we've seen in this chapter are not a list of how you should lead, nor are they a list of how you should be. Instead, they are a description of behaviours that emerge organically when your nervous system is calm and you operate from a position of unconditional worth.

You are not trying to *be* a better leader. In the fellow state, you are automatically more relaxed, cooperative, understanding and compassionate. When you lead from that state, then your actions are better for your team, relationships and work performance. You have more energy and your natural enthusiasm for your work and your leadership role emerges.

The ripple effect of a leader's belief in their own unconditional worth is huge, but this impact is not limited to the workplace. In the next chapter, we explore what happens in greater ripples with people and situations.

NINE

Beyond Imposter Syndrome

*I*n my final conversation with James, we reviewed his whole journey of getting rid of imposter syndrome and developing unconditional worth. To start, I asked him how his past week had gone.

'Calm and not very busy,' he replied. 'A quiet week.'

It was Friday afternoon and he was relaxed and looking forward to enjoying the weekend with his young family. When I asked more about the week's events, James revealed he'd done two board-level presentations. Previously, he would have gone into overdrive, over-preparing and working long, anxious hours. This time, James prepared well in advance. Then, knowing he had prepared enough, he switched off the night before.

One of these presentations was for a new client and a deal worth 30% of his team's sales for next year. Such a high-stakes presentation would have meant at least two nights of lost sleep for James in the past. This time, he slept well and woke refreshed and ready for the meeting.

A junior member of the team came with him to the meeting. Previously, James would have been beside himself with worry and would have largely ignored her presence. Instead, in the thirty minutes before the meeting started, he talked through the details of the presentation, answered her concerns and discussed how she would frame her responses to some of the technical questions that would come her way.

In short, James instinctively mentored her now that he had the mental space to do so. His nervous system communicated that he was relaxed, which meant that her nervous system could relax too. James was delighted that he could now act as the kind of good role model he had always admired.

In both meetings, James was calm, comfortable and in flow. When someone threw him a curveball, he didn't miss a beat. In fact, he was thrilled by the challenge, handled it well and enjoyed the meeting, seeing it as a stimulating discussion. In the past, he would have spent hours worrying and another sleepless night afterwards, replaying the meeting in his head.

This was the same week in which Tom had had the outburst we saw in the previous chapter. In the past, James would have been reeling from it for days, but this time he took quick action, and then moved on with his day undisturbed.

'Oh, and another thing,' James said, grinning. 'I delegated more of the work to the rest of my team this week. Before, I was doing all the important things myself and didn't trust them to do these things well enough.

'The team loved getting their teeth into a good challenge. I'm pleased to say I didn't once micromanage. I'd have done that before, even though I always hated when I did it. My team did well with just a little guidance from me and I have so much more time on my hands as a result. I'm even going to finish at 4.30pm today, so I can spend a little more time with my family this evening.'

By this time, we were laughing because the week had not been quiet at all for the 'old James'. The week was not uneventful, but James himself was calm and so it felt like a quiet week to him. The old imposter behaviours and thinking had evaporated, and James was enjoying his work and his leadership. Finally, he was feeling that he was good enough.

The ripple effects

A research study published in 2021 explored how people think creatively.[59] The test was for people to create a specific structure from a group of blocks. Most tried to solve the problem by adding more blocks, but the elegant and simple solution was to remove some of the blocks. Few people even thought about that.

The researchers noted that when people are under time pressure, they are even less likely to think about subtraction. Of course, you now know why these people were less creative under stress.

I see this with imposter syndrome too. Most people see the surface symptoms and think that the solution must be to add something. That they should get more confidence, build a more involved morning routine or add mindset techniques, for example, when the simple, elegant solution to imposter syndrome is subtraction: remove the underlying cause.

When you do this, it's like removing a weight that had been holding down a balloon. The balloon naturally and effortlessly soars.

Without imposter syndrome, your inherent emotional intelligence, leadership, creativity, productivity, resilience and authenticity shine through. When you finally feel good enough, you relish your work and enjoy seeing just how far you can go. However, the effects of developing unconditional worth extend much further than the workplace and impact how you show up in the world, your relationships and contribution.

Personality

Helen had had therapy years ago for a crisis event, and since then had checked in with her therapist twice a year. Twenty years on, Helen's therapist knew she didn't need more therapy, but he did suggest that she come to me for some assistance.

She was sabotaging her high-profile consulting business, had huge self-doubt and was definitely suffering from imposter syndrome. In our work together, Helen took huge leaps forward in her self-belief and self-acceptance, became much calmer, dialled down her stress and anxiety, and happily stepped up to speak at conferences that would have been torture for her in the past.

Towards the end of our work together, Helen had her next check-in with her therapist. They chatted for a while, and then he burst out, 'You are dramatically different in how you talk about your business and yourself!'

It was obvious to Helen how much of a transformation she'd made, but she was pleased to get an unsolicited opinion to confirm it. Especially from an expert who had known her for so long.

'I don't feel like a different person,' said Dagen, CEO of a large New York hedge fund, when he'd completed his own journey to unconditional worth. 'I thought this process would change my personality, but it's only changed how I see and react to events and think about myself.'

Dagen is not alone in his initial worry that the process might change his personality, because he thought that imposter syndrome was a part of his personality. Dagen's surprise at how he could have huge shifts in his thinking and behaviour and still feel like the same person is not unusual either.

This confirms the statement I made at the beginning of this book: imposter syndrome is *not* your personality. Eliminating it reveals more of your true inner qualities because the negativity and stress of imposter syndrome are removed.

Gary, a professional services partner, had previously thought he was shy. This is a strong, clear label and one he was unhappy with, but had resigned himself to. Once he'd learned how to accept others, and then himself, he noticed that he was relaxed and naturally interacted more with others. He found himself chatting merrily with the waitress at lunch one day and realised that he would never have done that in the past.

This is not a change in his personality, but the result of a calmer nervous system. Shyness sometimes includes the compensating behaviour of running. Gary would previously not have spoken to the waitress and withdrawn from interacting. Now that he was more often in the fellow state, he generally saw people as safer. He no longer needed the waitress's approval or to avoid her disapproval. He now felt connected to her, and his natural warmth and interest in people emerged.

This was Gary connecting with who he really is, since the belief in conditional worth was no longer colouring his interactions. Without having to repeatedly remind himself, he was becoming more authentic due to what he'd let go of. Needless to say, Gary was thrilled to uncover more of his real self.

Relationships

The toll of imposter syndrome is frequently paid in relationships, both personal and business ones.

Remember Kim, the CEO from Chapter 2 who was stuck in the endless loop of the fight state? Her turn-around point in the whole process was realising that she had been responding to perceived attacks that had nothing to do with her. Her amygdala had previously been on hyper-alert, seeing danger where there was none.

With this realisation, she was quickly able to stay calm in situations that would have made her defensive in the past. It changed the whole tone of the meetings she was in, how she worked with peers and even interacted at business social events. As she developed unconditional worth, this calm became easier and easier for her to achieve.

Matt, Managing Director of a UK sportswear manufacturer, knew imposter syndrome was the cause of his divorce. His chronic over-preparing had meant he worked extremely long hours, was constantly distracted and couldn't switch off. He had been unable to be present with his ex-wife physically, mentally or emotionally. Before he started to address his imposter syndrome, his new partner was also threaten-ing to leave, with exactly the same complaints as his ex-wife.

Learning how to accept himself without the demand to be perfect put a halt to Matt's over-preparing. It gave him time to get calm, relax and switch off, which meant he was more present and able to enjoy himself when he was with his new partner. He was spending his time and energy wisely on things he wanted to do rather than the wasted cycle of over-preparing and stress.

Having switched to the fellow state, you automatically become more open, considerate, kind and willing to help people around you. You now have the ability to accept others when they make a mistake and accept yourself when you make a mistake. Relationships of all kinds become more relaxed, enjoyable and filled with acceptance and understanding.

Parenting

When I explain how conditional worth is developed, I see many parents run the gauntlet of self-criticism, judgement and fear of having hurt their children.

'How could we have done something so awful?' they often ask.

Firstly, you teach your children beliefs that you were taught. Since you were never taught a belief in your own unconditional worth, how could you teach it to your children? You didn't know it existed. Plus, as it is an unconscious belief, it wouldn't even have occurred to you to look at it. You couldn't see it.

If you're a parent, you can relax and accept that you have done the best you could with the resources you had. Now that you have more knowledge about conditional worth, you can pay attention and start to do things differently.

Parenting with unconditional worth could fill many books.[60] Although the topic is well beyond the scope of this book, there are several things a parent can do quickly to help foster unconditional worth.

Don't label your child as good or bad in response to things they have done, not done, said or not said. Label the action, but not the child doing it.

Don't be your child's judge. Encourage them to develop their own authority by asking them what they liked about something they did, what they learned from it or whether they had fun doing it.

Teaching children means creating boundaries and enforcing them, but there is a difference between punishment and consequences. Punishment involves *your* emotions, such as anger, disappointment or fear. Consequences are the natural result of your child breaking a rule that you, as a parent, enforce. When you apply consequences without disapproval (and judgement) of them, it means you are teaching your child that there is a difference between who they are and what they do.

However, just like airlines recommend that you put on your own oxygen mask before helping others, the biggest difference you can make for your children is to develop your own unconditional worth. Parents model their beliefs in hundreds of ways every day in what they say and do, how they talk about the world, how they talk about themselves, and their actions.

Your congruent modelling of unconditional worth will have the greatest impact on your child. They will naturally adopt your beliefs, accepting others and themselves.

Spirituality

Even though we have addressed developing unconditional worth from the practical standpoint of imposter syndrome, high performance and neuroscience, the impact of this change ripples out to all parts of your life, including your spiritual life.

Geoff had been a regular meditator for over twenty years, but he criticised himself for still not being able to sit undistracted and peaceful every time, or for getting up off his meditation cushion feeling calm, only to go straight back into the drama and stress around him. It didn't seem to stick.

Geoff saw the letting-go process as a systematic way to develop the non-attachment and compassion that are at the heart of his meditation practice. He also found he could do letting-go in the moment as events unfolded. This meant that he was now able to live his non-attachment ideal throughout each day.

As an active Christian, Luke had always struggled with forgiving people. He'd been taught that he should forgive others and that this would make him a good person, but he'd never learned how to actually do it. He just didn't seem to be able to let things go, so Luke judged himself as 'bad' for it, reinforcing the belief that he was not good enough.

When Luke learned step-by-step how to forgive, he jumped into it with enthusiasm. Years of slights, irritations and victimhood fell away, which deepened his feelings of peace and kindness. He felt more like he belonged and felt closer to God.

Every major religion in the world recommends peace, kindness, compassion and forgiveness. They teach that forgiveness and acceptance lead to freedom from suffering and improve connection with a higher power, however the faithful define that.

The usual instruction is to *be* more of those qualities. Unfortunately, few religions teach exactly how to achieve them because they don't know how. Letting go as described in this book results in a huge step towards these spiritual ideals because you drop blame, self-doubt, judgement and victimhood and foster compassionate acceptance of others.

Performance

Finally, we come full circle to imposter syndrome at work. The process in this book makes you more productive in your job since you're no longer wasting precious time over-preparing or ruminating.

It makes you more focused because you're no longer distracted by nagging thoughts in your head or by worrying about what others are thinking of you. You become more present and relaxed, which opens up your mind to finding creative and cooperative solutions to problems. You feel like you belong in your role, in your team and in business, which makes your work satisfying, easier and more enjoyable. You have more energy, sleep better and often start taking better care of yourself, which gives you the capacity to perform at your peak level regularly.

Sometimes, people worry that if they are relaxed and happy like this, then they will stop being motivated to achieve great things. There is a common misconception that pain is the only motivator for success in business. While pain is excellent at motivating, the cost is also high in terms of energy, focus and productivity, with a toll on relationships, family and enjoyment of your life and work.

Pain is only one motivator, however. The other natural motivator is the adventurer or explorer in you. The one who wants to try new things just to see if they will work. The one thrilled to stretch a little more to see if you can do it. The flow state is reached when you are working at the smallest of stretches. Then, high performance becomes a joy and the positive feedback encourages you to try the next little stretch.

My experience of watching scores of high performers develop unconditional worth is that they don't slow down, get lazy or drop out. I see the opposite, in fact. They are energised and naturally step forward, making bigger and bolder moves. Frequently, they step up into industry leadership roles as well, following their desire to contribute and make a significant difference.

As you can see, we've moved beyond imposter syndrome. Imposter syndrome is merely the symptom of a belief in conditional worth. The belief that Carl Rogers identified seventy years ago as the root cause of unhappiness and suffering.

Eliminating your imposter syndrome by cultivating your sense of unconditional worth is therefore the ultimate journey in self-development and transformation. You develop peace, effortless confidence and limitless possibilities, all of which are your birthright as a human.

Resources

The big messages from *Outsmart Imposter Syndrome* are that imposter syndrome is not who you are, you are not alone and there is something you can do about it.

Here are further resources to help you manage or eliminate imposter syndrome for good.

1. Quiz

Take the free quiz to see how much imposter syndrome affects you: www.outsmartimpostersyndrome.com/quiz

2. Outsmart Imposter Syndrome Online Course

This is a private, workshop-style online course to build your own set of personalised tools to manage imposter syndrome, as described in Chapters 2–4. Typical results are feeling calmer, lighter and more in control. For details, www.outsmartimpostersyndrome.com/course

3. Inner Success

Inner Success is the flagship one-to-one programme to eliminate imposter syndrome for good by developing unconditional worth over 8–12 weeks.

This is the full transformation that creates freedom from imposter syndrome and freedom from the suffering that conditional worth creates.

For more details of this programme working with Tara or one of her team of Inner Success coaches, click the link here: www.outsmartimpostersyndrome.com/innersuccess

Notes

1   KJ Carpenter, *The History of Scurvy and Vitamin C* (Cambridge University Press, 1986)
2   E Brennan-Wydra, H.W Chung., N Angoff, J ChenFeng, A Pillips, J Schreiber, C Young and K Wilins, 'Maladaptive Perfectionism, Impostor Phenomenon, and Suicidal Ideation Among Medical Students', *Academic Psychiatry* 45, 708–715 (2021), https://doi.org/10.1007/s40596-021-01503-1
3   C Rogers, 'A theory of therapy, personality, and interpersonal relationships, as developed in the client-centered framework', in S Koch (ed), *Psychology; A Study of a Science, Volume 3: Formulations of the Person and the Social Context* (McGraw-Hill, 1959)
4   PR Clance and SA Imes, 'The imposter phenomenon in high achieving women: Dynamics and therapeutic interventions', *Psychotherapy*, 15/3 (1978), 241–247, https://doi.org/10.1037/h0086006
5   GM Matthews, 'Imposter phenomenon: Attributions for success and failure' (1984), paper presented at American Psychological Association, Toronto

6   D.M Bravata, S.A Watts, A.L Keefer, D.K Madhusudhan, K.T Taylor, D.M Clark, R.S Nelson, K.O Cokley and H.K Hagg, (2020) 'Prevalence, Predictors, and Treatment of Impostor Syndrome: a Systematic Review', *Journal of General Internal Medicine*, Apr;35(4):1252–1275 (2020), https://doi.org/10.1007/s11606-019-05364-1

7   T Halliday, 'A Validated Intervention for Imposter Syndrome', https://bit.ly/ValidatedMethod, accessed 21 February 2024

8   J Vergauwe, B Wille, M Feys, F De Fruyt, and F Anseel, 'Fear of being exposed: The trait-relatedness of the imposter phenomenon and its relevance in the work context', *Journal of Business and Psychology*, 30/3 (2015), 565–581, https://doi.org/10.1007/s10869-014-9382-5

9   J Hardt, *The Art of Smart Thinking* (Biocybernaut Press, 2007)

10   SW Porges, 'The polyvagal theory: New insights into adaptive reactions of the automatic nervous system', *Cleveland Clinic Journal of Medicine*, 76/Suppl 2 (2009), S86–S90, www.ccjm.org/content/76/4_suppl_2/S86, accessed 5 June 2023

11   T McClure, 'Jacinda Ardern resigns as Prime Minister of New Zealand', *The Guardian* (19 January 2023), www.theguardian.com/world/2023/jan/19/jacinda-ardern-resigns-as-prime-minister-of-new-zealand, accessed 5 June 2023

12   'Interview with Sir John Kirwan – Jacinda Ardern Ep5' *Open Minded Podcast*, https://youtu.be/MGKwczxm0pQ, accessed 5 June 2023

13   KA Cawcutt, P Clance, and S Jain, 'Bias, burnout, and imposter phenomenon: The negative impact of under-recognized intersectionality ', *Women's Health Reports*, 2/1 (2021), https://doi.org/10.1089/whr.2021.0138

14   T Halliday, *Unmasking: The coach's guide to imposter syndrome* (Rethink Press, 2018)

15   LJ Peter and R Hull, *The Peter Principle* (Pan Books, 1970)

16   J McCullough, 'The psychopathic CEO', *Forbes Magazine* (9 December 2019), www.forbes.com/sites/jackmccullough/2019/12/09/the-psychopathic-ceo, accessed 5 June 2023

17   S Fried-Buchalter, 'Fear of success, fear of failure, and the imposter phenomenon among male and female marketing managers', *Sex Roles*, 37 (1997), 847–859, https://doi.org/10.1007/BF02936343

18 D Waldman, D Wang, M Stikic, C Berka, PA Balthazard, T Richardson, NM Pless, and T Maak, 'Emergent leadership and team engagement: An application of neuroscience technology and methods', *Academy of Management 2013 Annual Meeting, AOM (2013)*, 632–637, www.researchgate.net/publication/259678311, accessed 5 June 2023

19 SW Porges, *The Polyvagal Theory: Neurophysiological foundations of emotions, attachment, communication, and self-regulation* (WW Norton, 2011)

20 H Benson, *The Relaxation Response* (William Morrow & Co, 2000 reprint)

21 A Mani, S Mullainathan, E Shafir, and J Zhao, 'Poverty impedes cognitive function', 341/6149 (2013), 976–980, www.science.org/doi/10.1126/science.1238041, accessed 5 June 2023

22 B McEwen and R Sapolsky, 'Stress and your health', *The Journal of Clinical Endocrinology & Metabolism*, 91/2 (2006), E2, https://doi.org/10.1210/jcem.91.2.9994

23 Mental Health Foundation, 'Stress: Are we coping?' (May 2018), www.mentalhealth.org.uk/explore-mental-health/publications/stress-are-we-coping-report, accessed 5 June 2023

24 Office for National Statistics, 'Adult drinking habits in Great Britain' (2018), www.ons.gov.uk/peoplepopulationandcommunity/healthandsocialcare/drugusealcoholandsmoking/datasets/adultdrinkinghabits, accessed 5 June 2023

25 D Goleman, *Emotional Intelligence: Why it can matter more than IQ* (Bloomsbury Publishing, 8 December 2020 reprint)

26 K Cherry, 'How the fight or flight response works', *The American Institute of Stress* (2019), www.stress.org/how-the-fight-or-flight-response-works, accessed 5 June 2023

27 S Haines, *Trauma Is Really Strange* (Singing Dragon, 2015)

28 In my previous writing, I have referred to this as the friend state. However, other writers have since used friend state to mean fawn, that is, trying to appease or befriend an attacker to avoid harm. To avoid any confusion, I use the fellow state to mean the social-engagement state, (although I'm tickled to have found another 'f' to continue the alliteration)

29 S Kotler, *The Rise of Superman: Decoding the science of ultimate human performance* (Quercus Publishing Ltd, 2014)

30 D Goleman, *Focus* (Bloomsbury Publishing Plc, 2013)

31 'Monzo CEO on death threats, depression and digital banking wars – Tom Blomfield Ep86', *Diary of a CEO* Podcast, www.youtube.com/watch?v=gP2_QOCrVO4, accessed 5 June 2023

32 Personal communication with a Swiss executive burnout clinic

33 J Vergauwe, B Wille, M Feys, F De Fruyt, and F Anseel, 'Fear of being exposed: The trait-relatedness of the imposter phenomenon and its relevance in the work context', *Journal of Business and Psychology*, 30/3 (2015), 565–581, https://doi.org/10.1007/s10869-014-9382-5

34 Tara Halliday (2016–2023): one-to-one interviews with over 700 executives about their imposter syndrome

35 A Clark, *Surfing Uncertainty* (Oxford University Press, 2016)

36 D Robson, *The Expectation Effect* (Canongate Books, 2022)

37 ME Raichle and DA Gusnard, 'Appraising the brain's energy budget', PNAS, 99/16 (2002), 10237–10239, https://doi.org/10.1073/pnas.172399499

38 C Rogers, 'A theory of therapy, personality, and interpersonal relationships, as developed in the client-centered framework', in S Koch (ed), *Psychology; A Study of a Science, Volume 3: Formulations of the Person and the Social Context* (McGraw-Hill, 1959)

39 Private conversation with Dr Greg Baer, 2016, who works exclusively with developing unconditional worth in adults. From observing over 10,000 people over several decades, he found only five who had grown up with the belief of unconditional worth. It provides a number to Dr Rogers' understanding of 'the vast majority'.

40 FW Stahnisch and R Nitsch, 'Santiago Ramón y Cajal's concept of neuronal plasticity: The ambiguity lives on' *Trends in Neurosciences*, 25/11 (2002), 589–591, https://doi.org/10.1016/S0166-2236(02)02251-8

41 MS Mahler, 'On the first three phases of the separation-individuation process', *International Journal of Psychoanalysis*, 53/3 (1972), 333–338, https://psycnet.apa.org/record/1973-20729-001, accessed 5 June 2023

42 G Baer, *Real Love and Post-Childhood Stress-Disorder* (Blue Ridge Press, 2010)

43 A Montagu, *Touching the Human Significance of the Skin* (HarperCollins, 1972)

44　A Fogel, 'Emotional and physical pain activate similar brain regions', *Psychology Today* (19 April 2012), www.psychologytoday.com/gb/blog/body-sense/201204/emotional-and-physical-pain-activate-similar-brain-regions, accessed 5 June 2023

45　Private communication, Greg Baer, 2016. His original work presented four survival strategies, but he later observed a fifth one, drama. I include drama to reflect his latest findings.

46　G Baer, *Real Love* (Blue Ridge Press, 2003)

47　JP Johansen, CK Cain, LE Ostroff, and JE LeDoux, 'Molecular mechanisms of fear learning and memory', *Cell*, 147/3 (2011), 509–524, https://doi.org/10.1016/j.cell.2011.10.009

48　S Davis, 'The human autonomic nervous system and emotional flashbacks', CPTSD Emotional Flashbacks (January 2021), https://cptsdfoundation.org/2021/01/18/the-human-autonomic-nervous-system-and-emotional-flashbacks, accessed 5 June 2023

49　A Morin, 'How cognitive reframing works', *Very Well Mind* (9 May 2023), www.verywellmind.com/reframing-defined-2610419, accessed 5 June 2023

50　SE Jankowitz, 'The victim-perpetrator paradigm', in *The Order of Victimhood*, Palgrave Studies in Compromise after Conflict (Palgrave Macmillan, 2018)

51　RB Crouse, K Kim, HM Batchelor, EM Girardi, R Kamaletdinova, J Chan, P Rajebhosale, ST Pittenger, LW Role, DA Talmage, M Jing, Y Li, X-B Gao, YS Mineur, and MR Picciotto, 'Acetylcholine is released in the basolateral amygdala in response to predictors of reward and enhances the learning of cue-reward contingency', *eLife* (18 September 2020), https://elifesciences.org/articles/57335, accessed 5 June 2023

52　MC Gonzaleza, JI Rossatoa, A Radiskea, LRM Bevilaquaa, and M Cammarota, 'Dopamine controls whether new declarative information updates reactivated memories through reconsolidation', *PNAS*, 118/29 (2021), e2025275118, www.pnas.org/doi/10.1073/pnas.2025275118, accessed 5 June 2023

53　D Osorio-Gómez, MI Miranda, K Guzmán-Ramos, and F Bermúdez-Rattoni, 'Transforming experiences: Neurobiology of memory updating/editing', *Frontiers*

in Systems Neuroscience, 17 (2023), www.frontiersin.org/
articles/10.3389/fnsys.2023.1103770/full, accessed 5 June
2023

54   B Ecker, 'Memory reconsolidation understood and
misunderstood', *International Journal of Neuropsychotherapy*,
3/1 (2015), 2–46, www.researchgate.net/
publication/270279444, accessed 5 June 2023

55   J Hu, Z Wang, X Feng, C Long, and D Schiller, 'Post-
retrieval oxytocin facilitates next day extinction of threat
memory in humans', *Psychopharmacology*, 236/1 (2019),
293–301, https://pubmed.ncbi.nlm.nih.gov/30370450,
accessed 5 June 2023

56   D Osorio-Gómez, MI Miranda, K Guzmán-Ramos, and F
Bermúdez-Rattoni, 'Transforming experiences: Neurobiology
of memory updating/editing', *Frontiers in Systems
Neuroscience*, 17 (2023), www.frontiersin.org/articles/10.3389/
fnsys.2023.1103770/full, accessed 5 June 2023

57   EJ Hermans, FP Battaglia, P Atsak, LD de Voogd, G
Fernández, and B Roozendaal, 'How the amygdala affects
emotional memory by altering brain network properties',
Neurobiology of Learning and Memory, 112 (2014), 2–16,
https://doi.org/10.1016/j.nlm.2014.02.005

58   P Eckman, *Emotions Revealed* (Orion, 2003)

59   GS Adams, BA Converse, AH Hales, and LE Klotz, 'People
systematically overlook subtractive changes', *Nature*, 592
(2021), 258–261, www.nature.com/articles/s41586-021-
03380-y, accessed 5 June 2023

60   G Baer, *Real Love in Parenting: Nine simple and powerfully
effective principles for raising happy and responsible children*
(Blue Ridge Press, 2005)

Acknowledgements

It takes a village to create a book and I'm delighted and grateful to have such great support. My heartfelt thanks to everyone involved.

It starts with Bethan and Glynis, encouraging me to set a date rather than writing my book 'sometime this year'. Then the Rethink Press team, Lucy, Joe, Kate, Anke, Alison and Eve for taking my words and turning them into a tangible book.

Then we have my fabulous beta readers Rachel, Areej, Marianne, Rebecca, Lucy, Andrew, David, Julie, Mike, Fanny, Jason and Robert for great feedback, asking excellent questions and ensuring I was making sense.

I'd also like to thank David for advice on legal and technical questions, and Lauren for adding polish. Thanks to my friends Alison, Alex, Erica, Kathryn and Julie for unending encouragement, and Fanny for limitless support with lovely long walks included. And finally for my mother, Irene, without whom this book would not be possible.

Finally, my deepest thanks to my teachers and all the researchers upon whose shoulders this work stands so strongly.

The Author

Tara Halliday is an Imposter Syndrome Specialist, trainer and international speaker.

She guides high-achieving leaders to eliminate imposter syndrome for good, and to develop energy, focus, calm resilience and effortless confidence.

Tara has a PhD in Engineering and over twenty years' experience as a qualified holistic therapist and certified Unconditional Worth Coach. Tara brings a practical and scientific approach to helping high performers reach their highest potential.

She is the author of Amazon #1 best-seller *Unmasking: The coach's guide to imposter syndrome.*

Her mission and passion are to free high achievers and leaders from unnecessary, internal suffering so they can live happy, meaningful, successful lives.

⊕ www.tarahalliday.com

⊕ www.completesuccess.co.uk

🖻 www.linkedin.com/in/tara-halliday-phd

🐦 https://twitter.com/tarahalliday1

Printed in Great Britain
by Amazon

56118855R10126